RECORDED VERSIONS
GUITAR

AUTHENTIC TRANSCRIPTIONS
WITH NOTES AND TABLATURE

UNLIMITED LOVE
RED HOT C

Music transcriptions by Pete Billmann and Jeff Jacobson

ISBN 978-1-7051-6940-7

HAL•LEONARD®

Visit Hal Leonard Online at
www.halleonard.com

World headquarters, contact:
Hal Leonard
7777 West Bluemound Road
Milwaukee, WI 53213
Email: info@halleonard.com

In Europe, contact:
Hal Leonard Europe Limited
42 Wigmore Street
Marylebone, London, W1U 2RY
Email: info@halleonardeurope.com

In Australia, contact:
Hal Leonard Australia Pty. Ltd.
4 Lentara Court
Cheltenham, Victoria, 3192 Australia
Email: info@halleonard.com.au

Black Summer

Words and Music by Anthony Kiedis, Flea, Chad Smith and John Frusciante

Tune down 1/2 step:
(low to high) Eb-Ab-Db-Gb-Bb-Eb

Intro
Moderately ♩ = 109

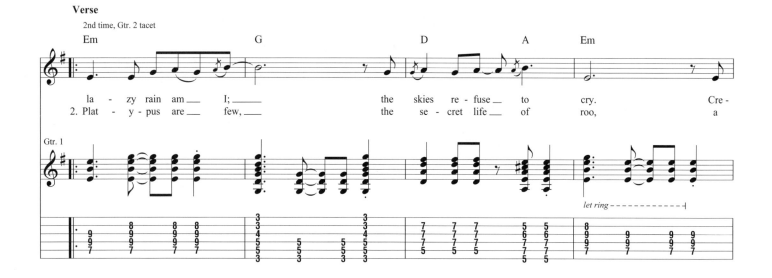

*Chord symbols reflect basic harmony.

Verse

2nd time, Gtr. 2 tacet

la - zy rain am ___ I; ___ the skies re - fuse ___ to cry. Cre - a
2. Plat - y - pus are ___ few, ___ the se - cret life ___ of roo, a

ma - tion takes ___ its piece of your sup - ply. ___ The
per - son - al - i - ty I nev - er knew. ___ Get it on. My

*T = Thumb on 6th string

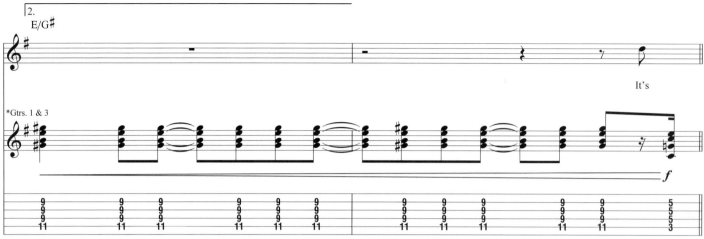

*Gtr. 3 (clean) w/ Leslie effect, played **mp**.
Composite arrangement

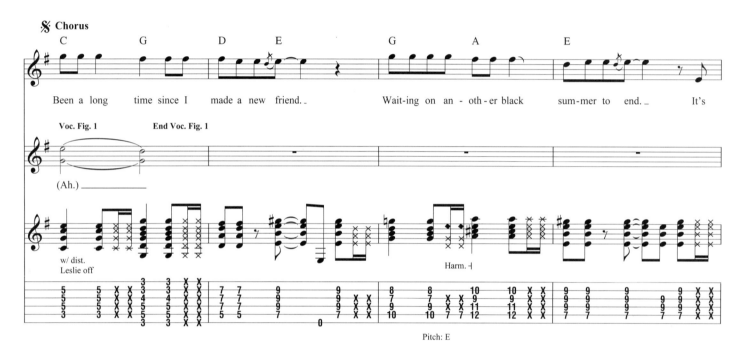

Guitar Solo

Gtrs. 1 & 3 tacet

*Chord symbols implied by bass.

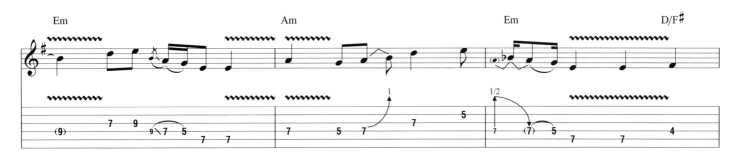

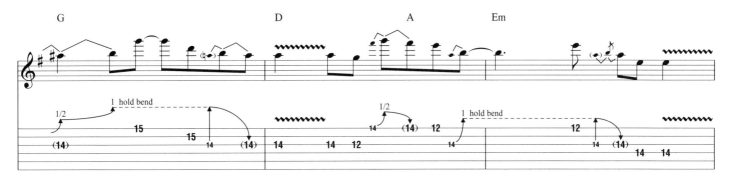

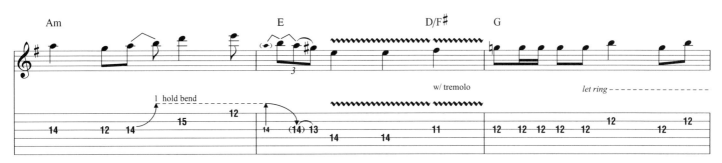

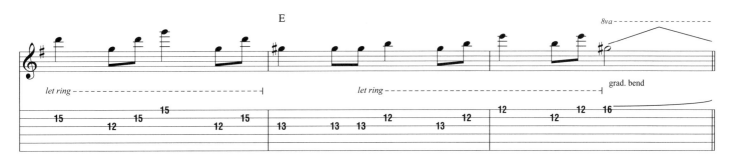

7

Verse

3. Crack the flam-ing ___ whip, ___ a, sail-ing on a cen-sor - ship.

D.S. al Coda

Rid-ing on a head-less horse to make the trip. ___ (It's)

*w/ echo set for quarter-note regeneration w/ 8 repeats.

⊕ Coda

Outro

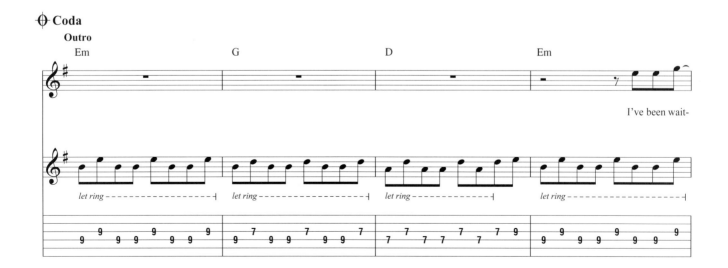

I've been wait-

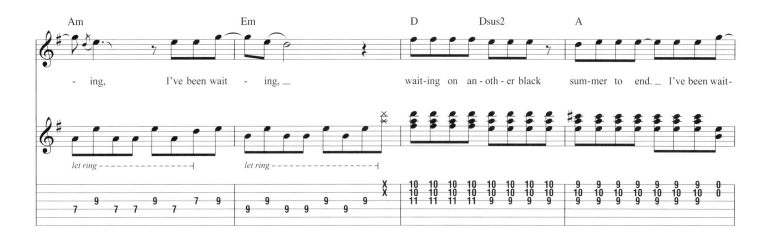

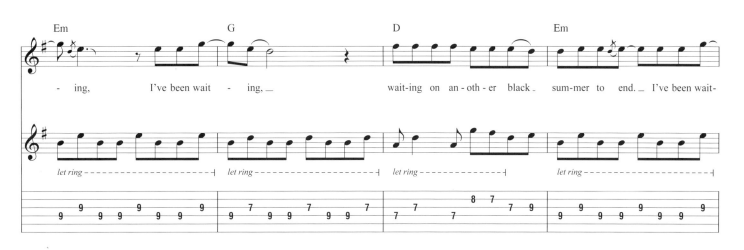

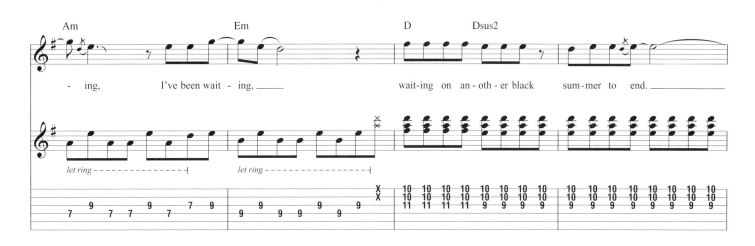

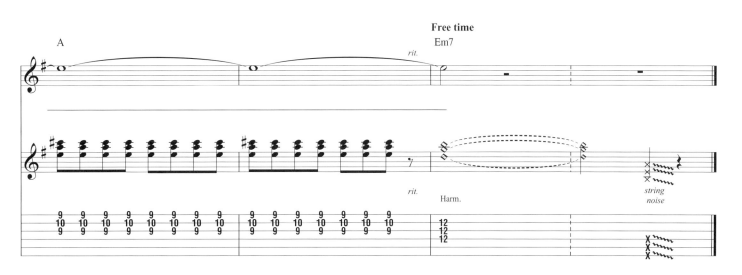

Here Ever After

Words and Music by Anthony Kiedis, Flea, Chad Smith and John Frusciante

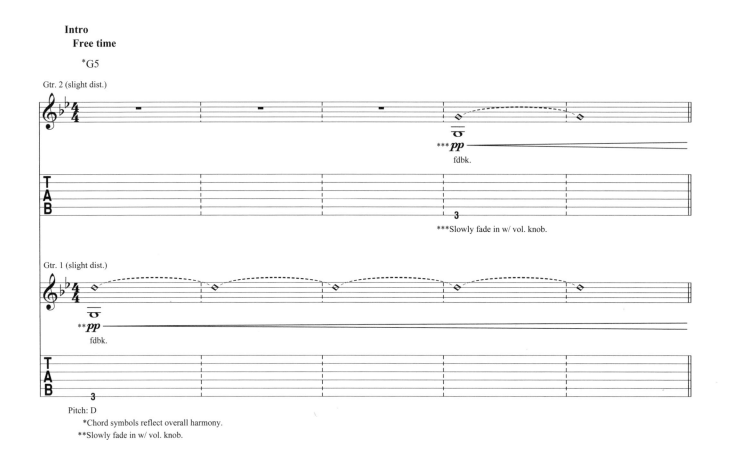

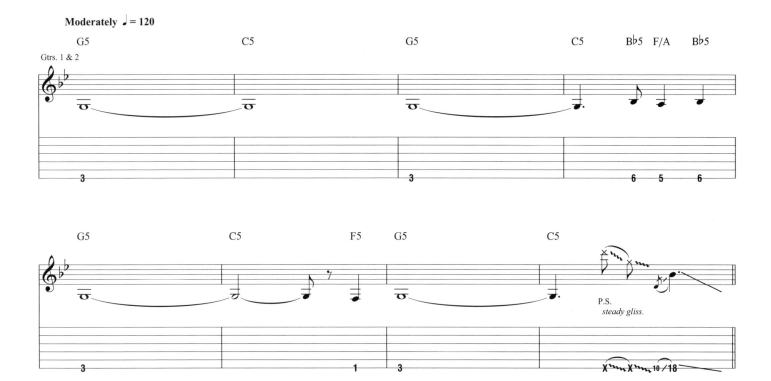

Chorus

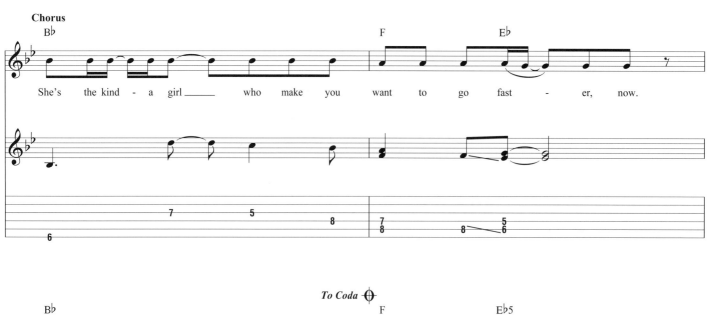

She's the kind-a girl _____ who make you want to go fast-er, now.

She's the kind-a girl _____ who make you steal your _ child. _____

Riff B   End Riff B

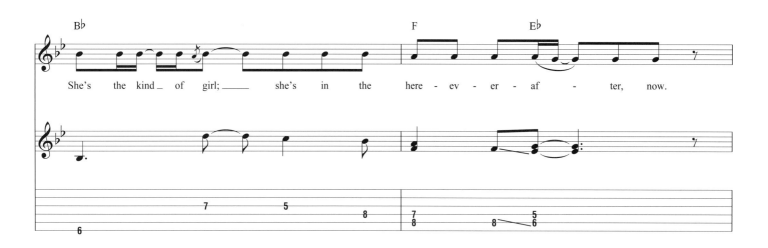

She's the kind_ of girl; _____ she's in the here-ev-er-af-ter, now.

There's a cry _ for help _____ and I don't   de-

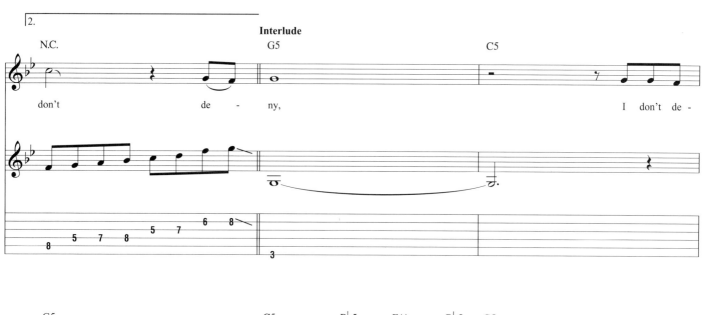

don't   de - ny,   I   don't de -

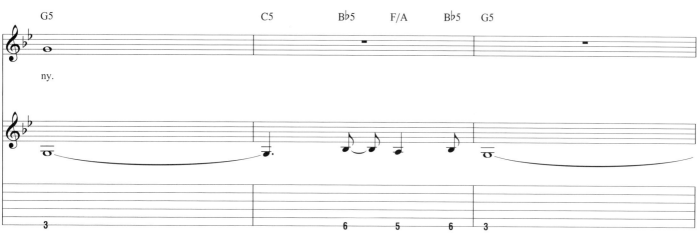

ny.

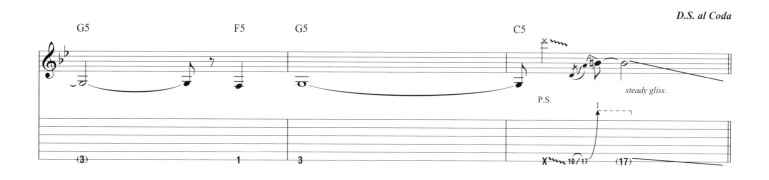

D.S. al Coda

steal   your _ child. ___   She's   the   kind _ of   girl; ___   she's   in   the

here - ev - er - af - ter, now. There's a cry__ for help__ and I don't de -

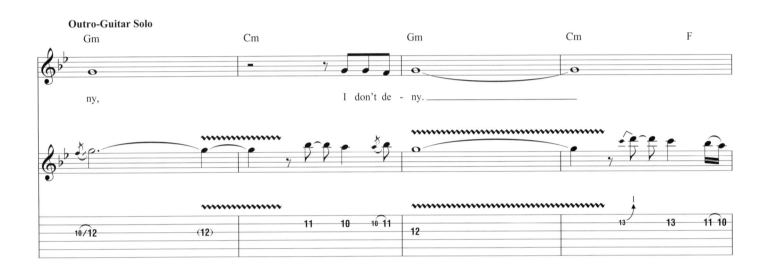

Outro-Guitar Solo

ny, I don't de - ny.__

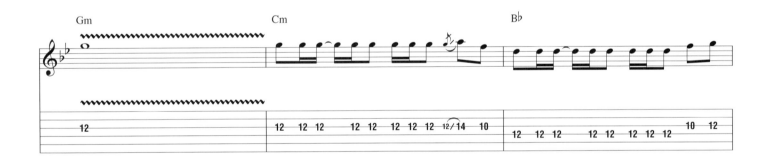

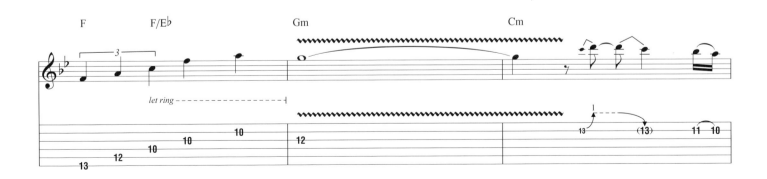

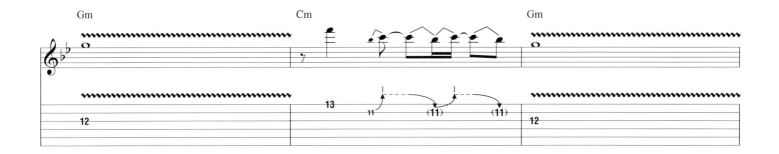

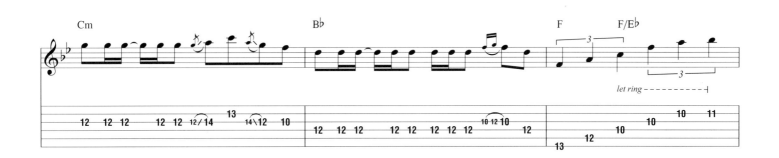

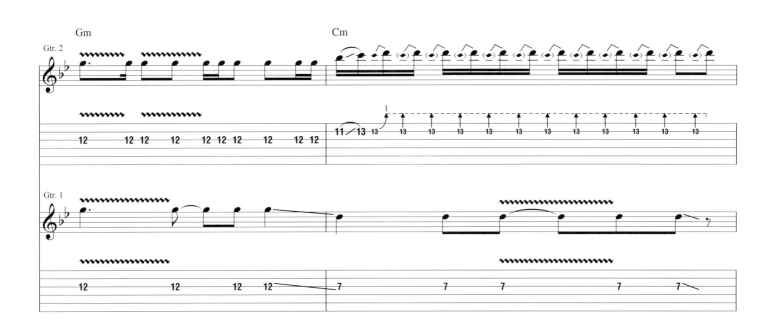

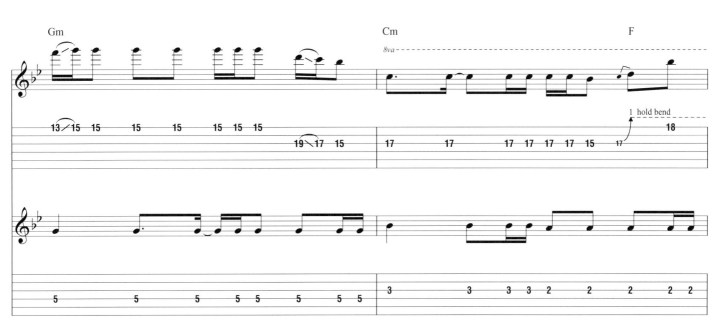

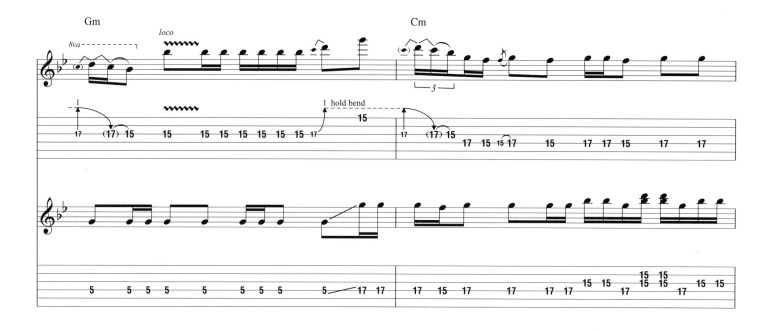

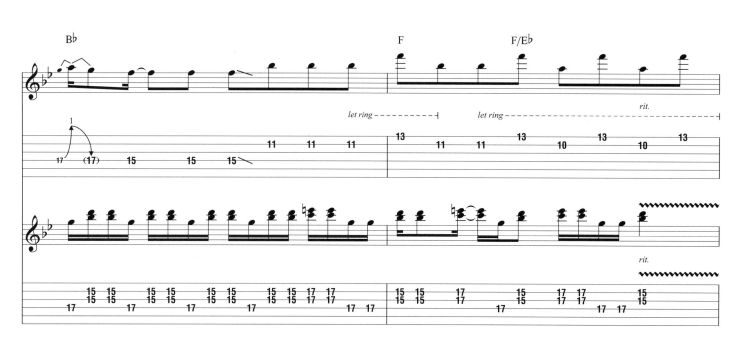

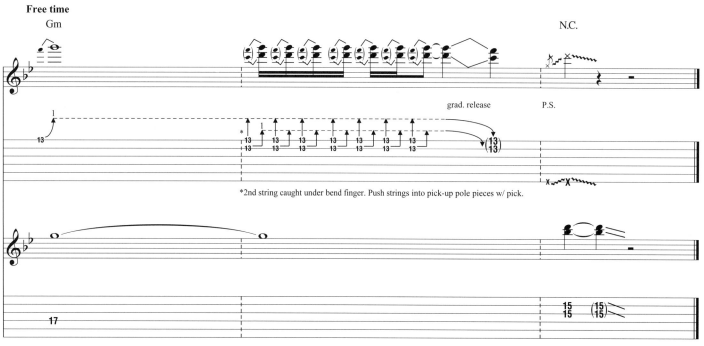

*2nd string caught under bend finger. Push strings into pick-up pole pieces w/ pick.

Aquatic Mouth Dance

Words and Music by Anthony Kiedis, Flea, Chad Smith and John Frusciante

Intro
Moderately ♩ = 100

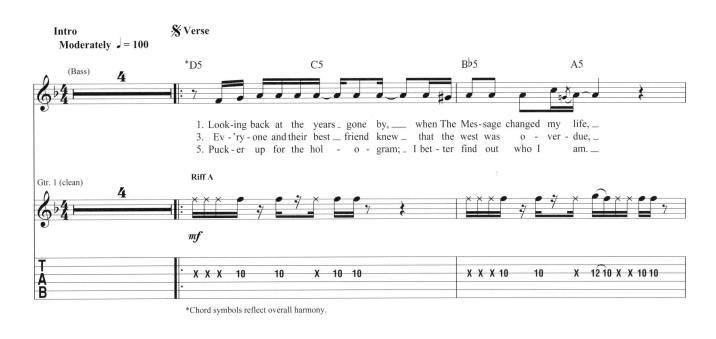

1. Look-ing back at the years gone by, ___ when The Mes-sage changed my life, ___
3. Ev-'ry-one and their best __ friend knew ___ that the west was o - ver-due, ___
5. Puck - er up for the hol - o - gram; ___ I bet - ter find out who I am. ___

Chord symbols reflect overall harmony.

heav - y met - al, the nest __ was dead, ___ well, and the rap - pers gave de - light. ___ But I don't know
grow-ing out of the fer - tile dirt, ___ well, and the cracks were fall - ing through. ___ But I don't know
Let it out with a down - town Scream, __ be-cause we need more space to jam. ___ But I don't know

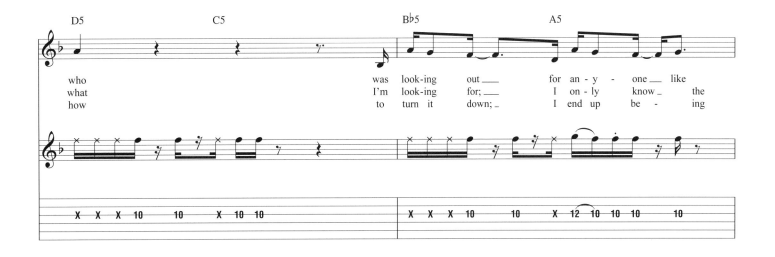

who ___ was look-ing out ___ for an - y - one ___ like
what ___ I'm look-ing for; ___ I on - ly know ___ the
how ___ to turn it down; ___ I end up be - ing

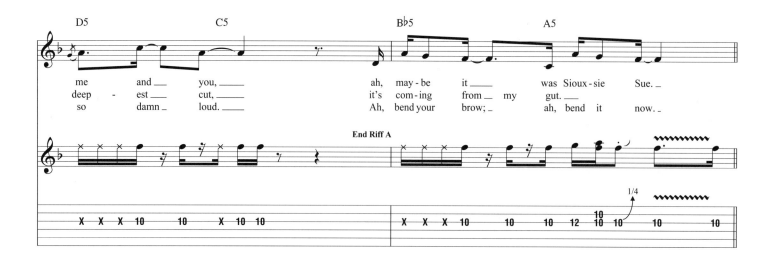

Verse

Gtr. 1: w/ Riff A

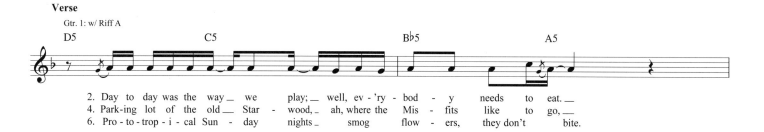

2. Day to day was the way__ we play;__ well, ev-'ry-bod - y needs to eat.__ And I don't know
4. Park-ing lot of the old __ Star - wood,__ ah, where the Mis - fits like to go,__ And I don't know
6. Pro - to - trop - i - cal Sun - day nights __ smog flow - ers, they don't bite.

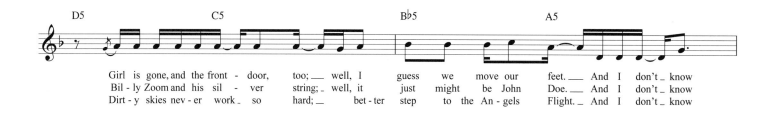

Girl is gone, and the front - door, too;__ well, I guess we move our feet.__ And I don't know
Bil - ly Zoom and his sil - ver string;__ well, it just might be John Doe.__ And I don't know
Dirt - y skies nev - er work __ so hard;__ bet - ter step to the An - gels Flight.__ And I don't know

To Coda ⊕

why the col - or of __ your eyes was sto - len from the __ sky, _____ and
where I'm gon - na sleep __ to - night. Please tell me, can you __ spare _____ a
if the em - bers of ____ my burn - ing flame _ are from this spliff. _ The

Chorus

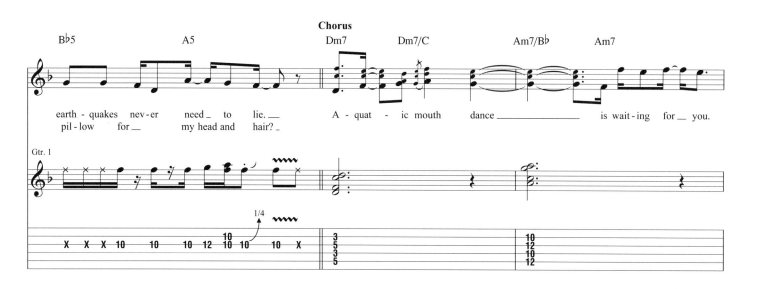

earth - quakes nev - er need _ to lie. __ A - quat - ic mouth dance _____ is wait - ing for __ you.
pil - low for __ my head and hair? _

Gtr. 1

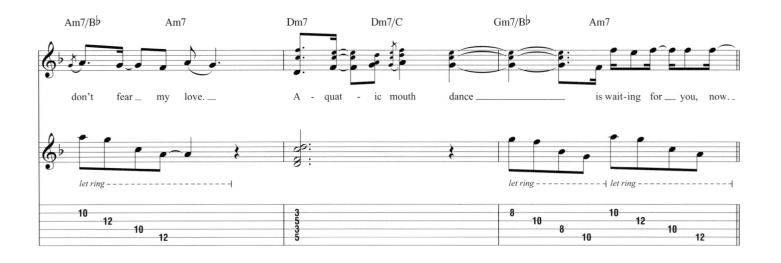

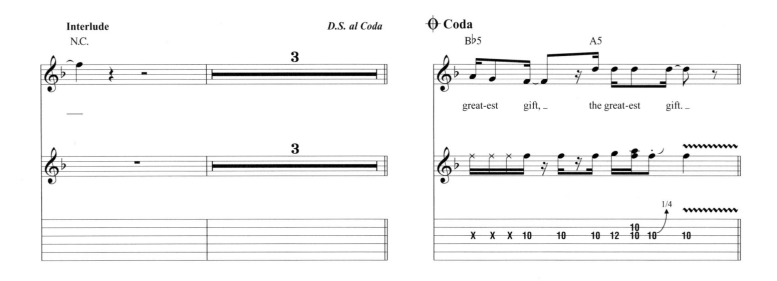

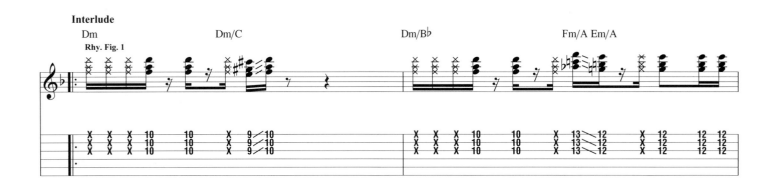

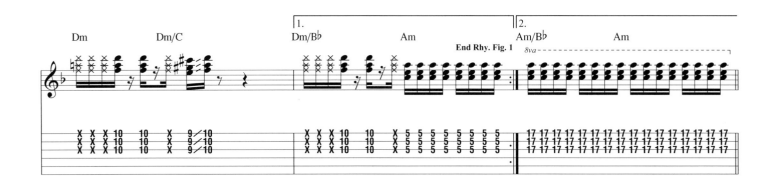

Verse

Gtr. 1: w/ Rhy. Fig. 1 (1 1/2 times)

7. Pep-pered up at the Cath - ay bash, ah, with a for - ty - five to split.

Spill-ing beer is a good foun - tain, ah, like the milk from a moth-er's tit. But I don't know

slow; ah, some - one has to come and teach me

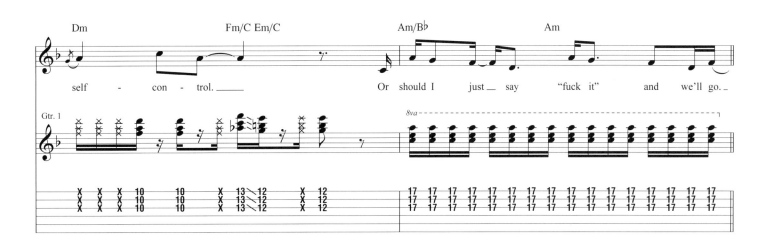

self - con - trol. Or should I just say "fuck it" and we'll go.

Outro

Gtr. 1: w/ Rhy. Fig. 1 (1 1/2 times)

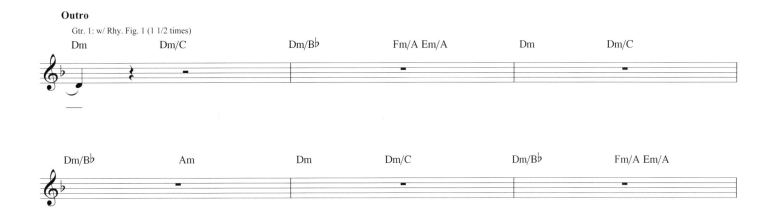

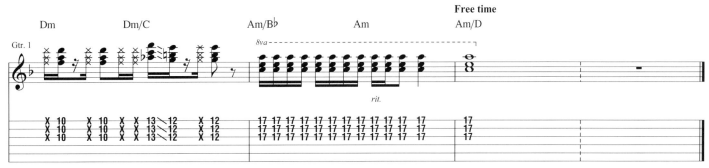

Not the One

Words and Music by Anthony Kiedis, Flea, Chad Smith and John Frusciante

*Doubled throughout

**Chord symbols reflect basic harmony.

***Vol. swells throughout

†Set for eighth-note regeneration w/ 1 repeat.

Lyrics:

1. I'm not the per - son that ___ you thought I was;
2. You see me as ___ the per - fect com - pli - ment,
3. I don't look like ___ my - self in pho - to - graphs;

I'm not the one ___ you thought ___ you knew.
you think that I'm ___ some - one to choose.
long days of time ___ have been ___ un - kind.

I'd do most an - y - thing ___ to make you think that I'm ___ the one. ___
You see me in ___ a way ___ that makes me want to re - in - vent ___
I miss the you, ___ the one ___ that makes me want to re - de - fine. ___

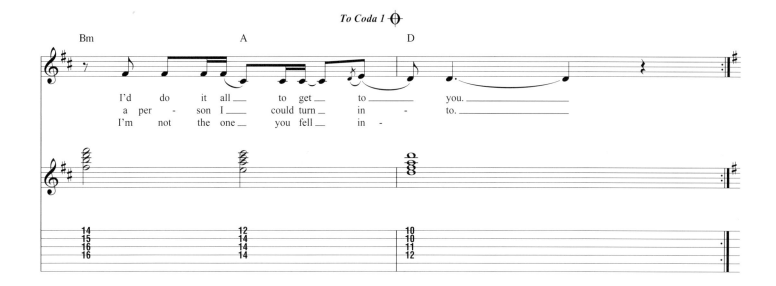

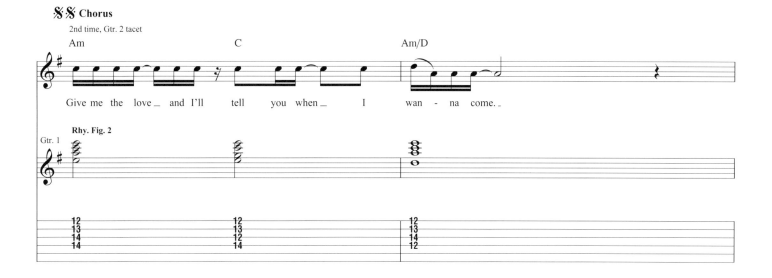

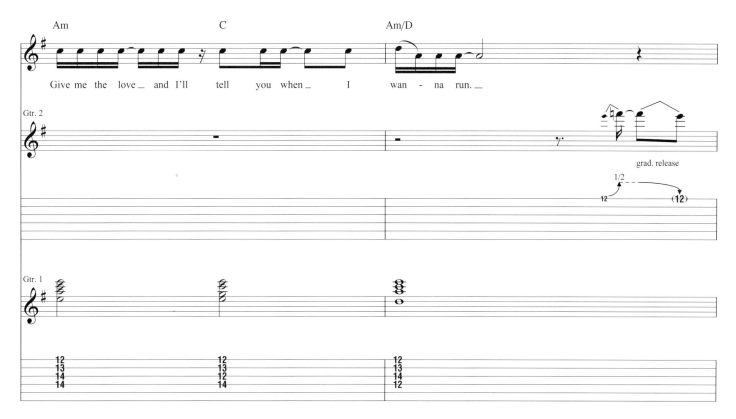

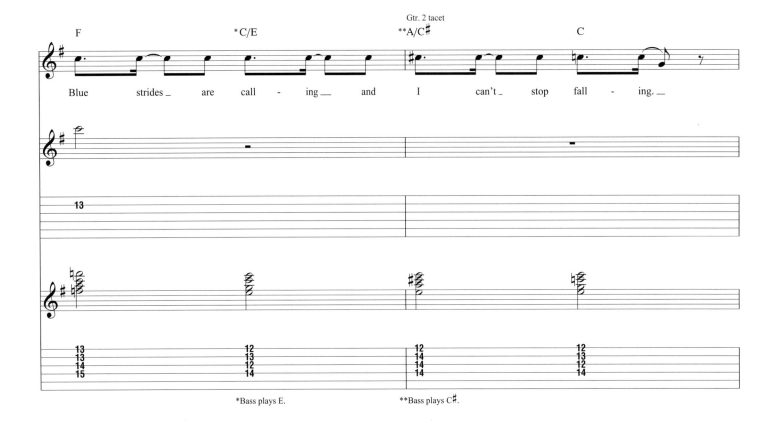

Blue strides are call - ing and I can't stop fall - ing.

*Bass plays E.   **Bass plays C#.

1st time, D.S. al Coda 1
(no repeat)
2nd time, To Coda 2 ⊕

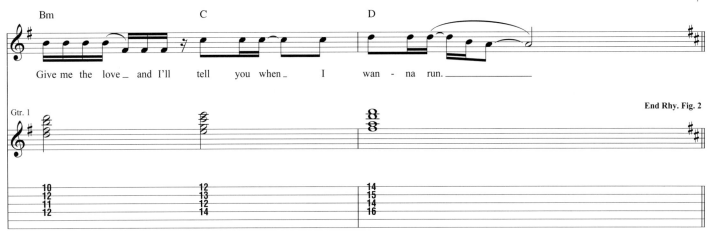

Give me the love and I'll tell you when I wan - na run.

Gtr. 1

End Rhy. Fig. 2

⊕ **Coda 1**

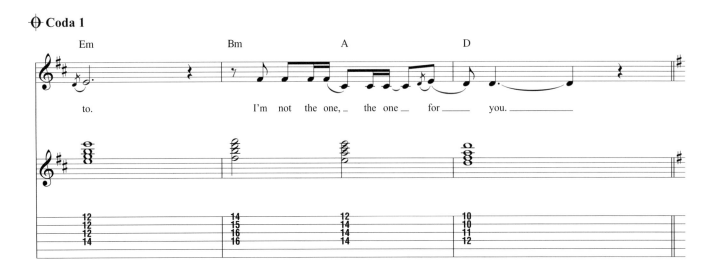

to.   I'm not the one, the one for you.

26

Chorus

Gtr. 1: w/ Rhy. Fig. 2

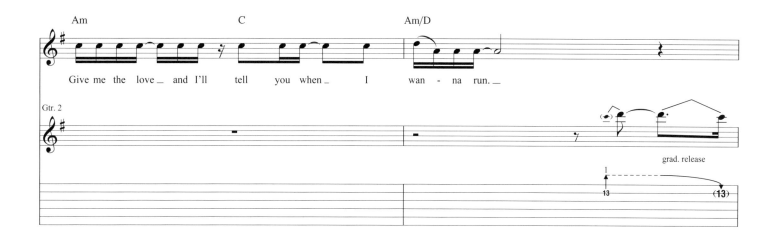

Give me the love __ and I'll tell you when __ I wan - na come. __

Give me the love __ and I'll tell you when __ I wan - na run. __

Gtr. 2

grad. release

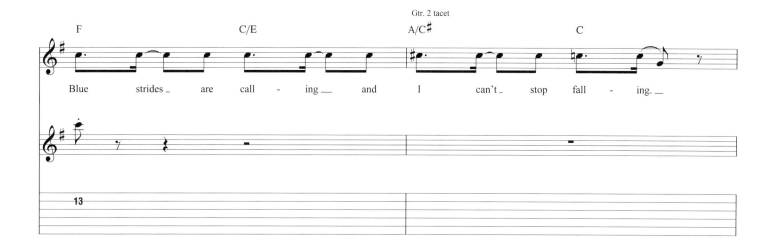

Gtr. 2 tacet

Blue strides __ are call - ing __ and I can't __ stop fall - ing. __

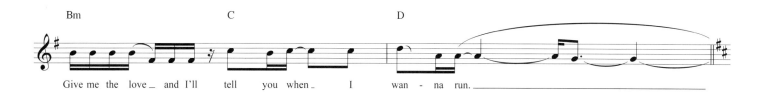

Give me the love __ and I'll tell you when __ I wan - na run. __

Guitar Solo

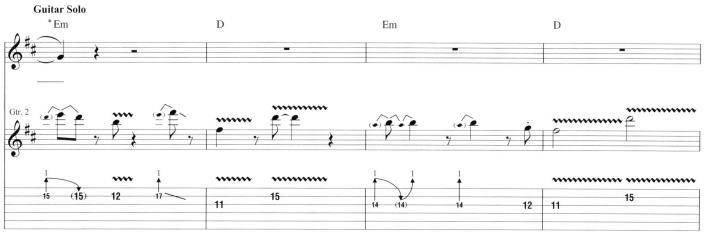

Gtr. 2

*Chord symbols reflect overall harmony.

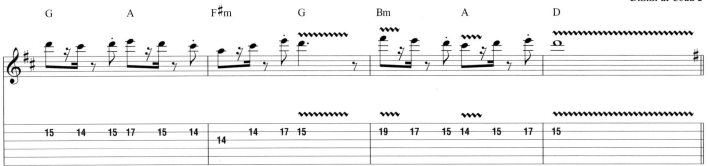

Coda 2

Outro-Guitar Solo

Gtr. 1: w Rhy. Fig. 1

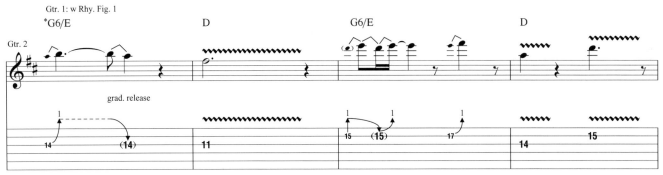

*Chord symbols reflect overall harmony.

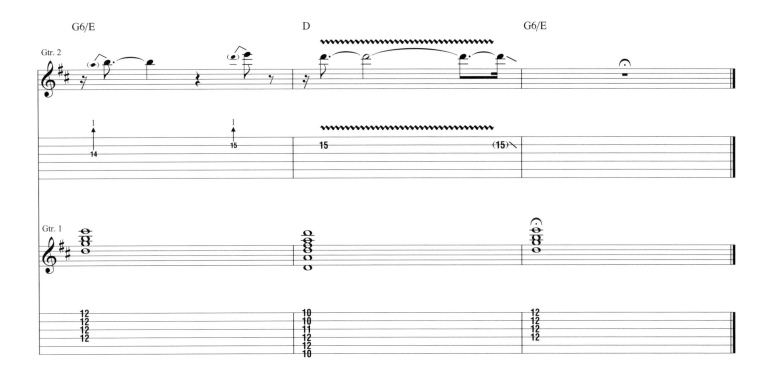

Poster Child

Words and Music by Anthony Kiedis, Flea, Chad Smith and John Frusciante

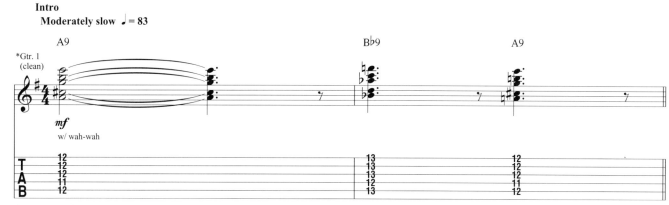

*Two gtrs. arr. for one.

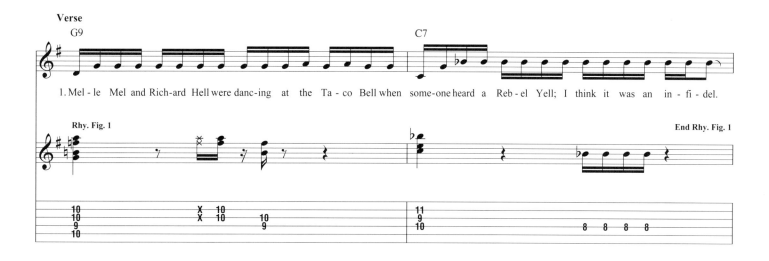

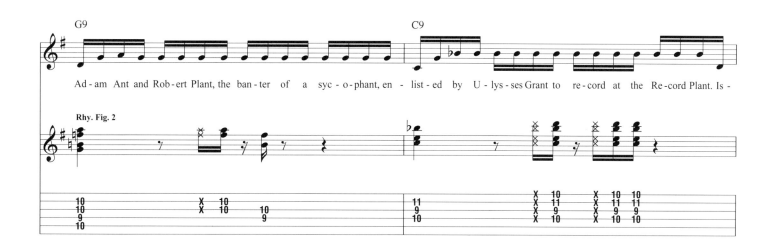

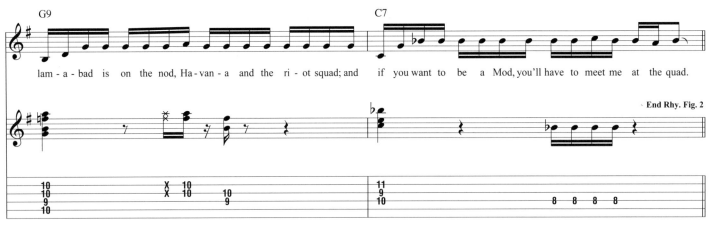

lam - a - bad is on the nod, Ha - van - a and the ri - ot squad; and if you want to be a Mod, you'll have to meet me at the quad.

End Rhy. Fig. 2

Post-Verse

Gtr. 1: w/ Rhy. Fig. 2

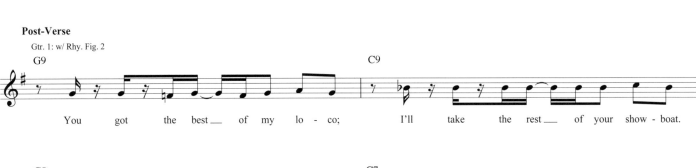

You got the best __ of my lo - co; I'll take the rest __ of your show - boat.

You got the best __ of my Yo - ko; I'll take the rest __ of your low note.

Verse

Gtr. 1: w/ Rhy. Fig. 2

2. Par - lia - ment's "A - tom - ic Dog," the hats were fill - ing up with fog; a talk a - bout the life and death of ev - 'ry pen - ny an - a - logue. The

Riff A

Gtr. 2 (slight dist.)

*Set for sixteenth-note regeneration w/ 1 repeat.

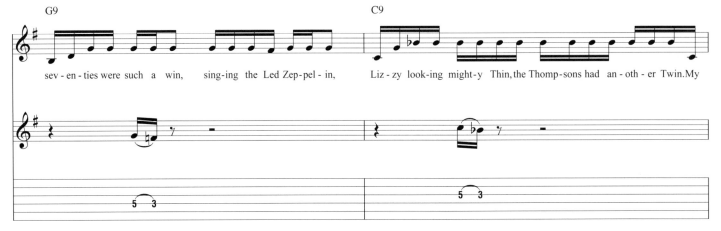

sev - en - ties were such a win, sing - ing the Led Zep - pel - in, Liz - zy look - ing might - y Thin, the Thomp - sons had an - oth - er Twin. My

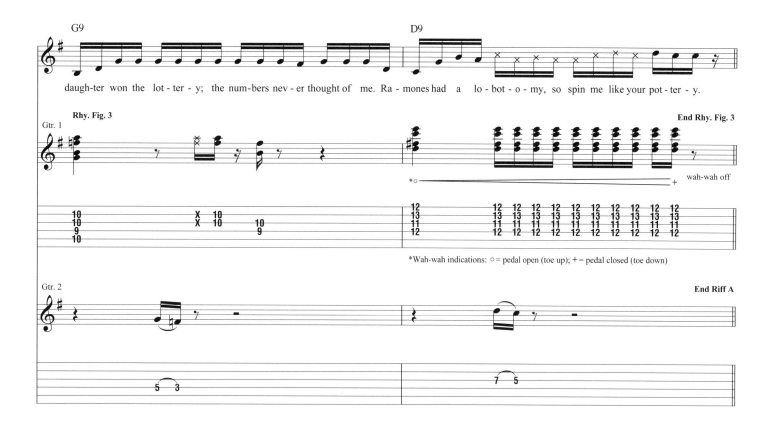

daugh-ter won the lot-ter - y; the num-bers nev - er thought of me. Ra - mones had a lo - bot - o - my, so spin me like your pot - ter - y.

*Wah-wah indications: ○ = pedal open (toe up); + = pedal closed (toe down)

Chorus

I will be your post-er child,_ ya know, the world is ours for a lit-tle while._ And then,

I will be your post-er child_ to - night._____ And, oh, la, da, da, da, ba,_ ba, ba, dum. 3. A

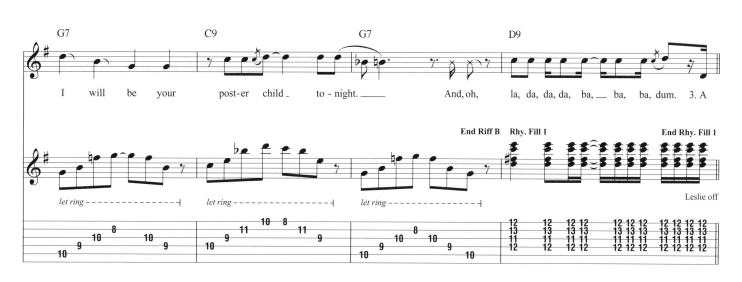

Verse

Gtr. 1: w/ Rhy. Fig. 1

funk-y feast of San-din-is-ta, ne-on mon-o Mo-na Li-sa; Ju-das Priest, the sweet ba-ris-ta, moth-er load was named Ter-e-sa.

Gtr. 1: w/ Rhy. Fig. 2

Bub-ble gum, I cum Ba-zoo-ka, Dirt-y Dan, Dean and De-lu-ca; smoked ba-nan-a in your hoo-kah, now I know the brand is RV-CA.

Ber-nie Mac and Cad-dy-shack were dust-y as the brick-er-brac, and if you ask me for the time, I'll tell you that the Fu-ture's Back.

Gtr. 2

*w/ octaver

octaver off

*Set for one octave lower.

Post-Verse

Gtr. 1: w/ Rhy. Fig. 2

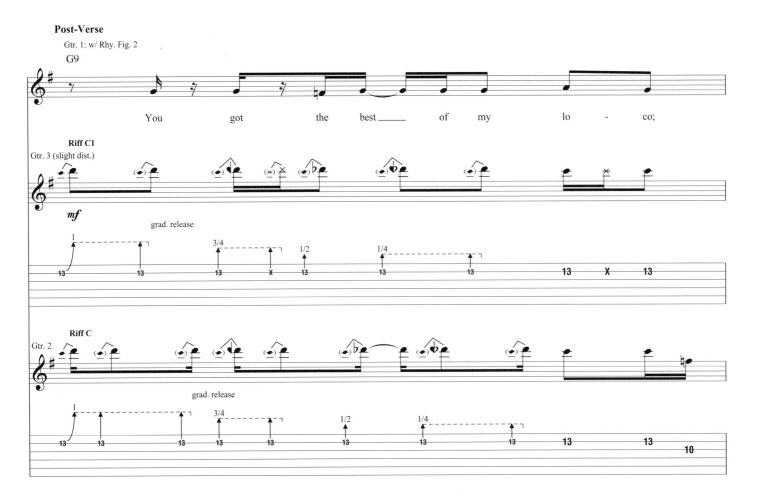

You got the best ____ of my lo - co;

Riff C1

Gtr. 3 (slight dist.)

mf

grad. release

Riff C

Gtr. 2

grad. release

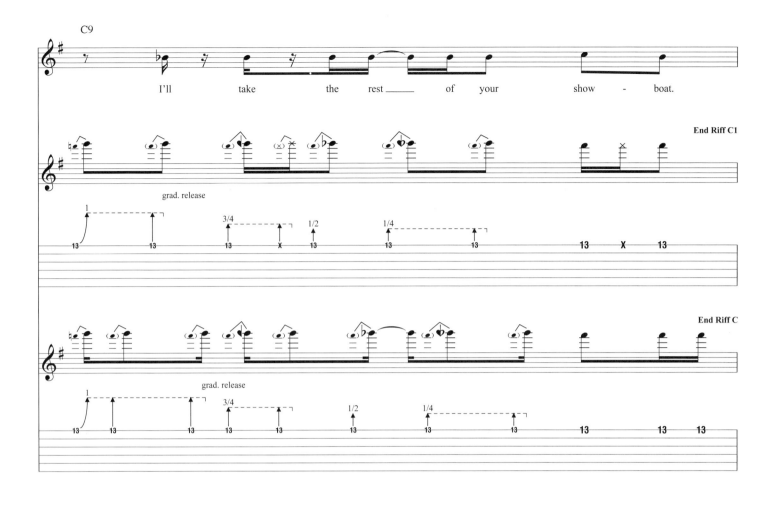

C9

I'll take the rest ____ of your show - boat.

End Riff C1

grad. release

End Riff C

grad. release

Gtrs. 2 & 3: w/ Riffs C & C1

G9   C7

You got the best ___ of my Yo - ko; I'll take the rest ___ of your low note. 4. Steve

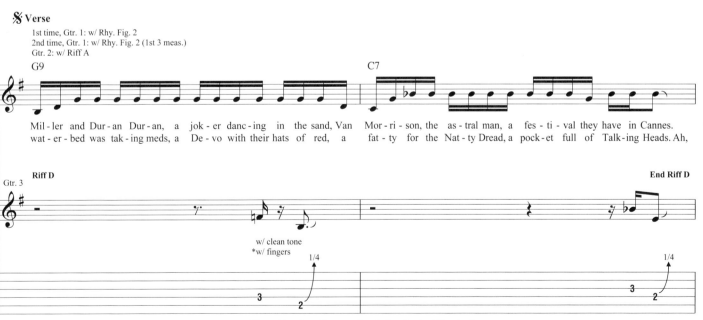

%𝄋 Verse

1st time, Gtr. 1: w/ Rhy. Fig. 2
2nd time, Gtr. 1: w/ Rhy. Fig. 2 (1st 3 meas.)
Gtr. 2: w/ Riff A

G9   C7

Mil - ler and Dur - an Dur - an, a jok - er danc - ing in the sand, Van Mor - ri - son, the as - tral man, a fes - ti - val they have in Cannes.
wat - er - bed was tak - ing meds, a De - vo with their hats of red, a fat - ty for the Nat - ty Dread, a pock - et full of Talk - ing Heads. Ah,

Riff D   End Riff D
Gtr. 3

w/ clean tone
*w/ fingers

*Snap strings by pulling away from fretboard and quickly releasing.

Gtr. 3: w/ Riff D

2nd time, Gtr. 1: w/ Rhy. Fill 3

G9 / C9

Speak of Chic-o and the Man, the Si-lence of a cer-tain Lamb; M - C - Five "Kick Out the Jam," a pon-cho full of con-tra-band.
Ma-ya's mak-ing pa-per planes, Ad-dic-tion to the days of Jane's; my Slur-pee's made of Pur-ple Rain, ten fin-gers in the li-on's mane.

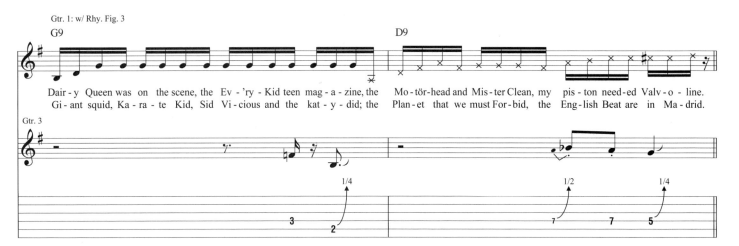

Gtr. 1: w/ Rhy. Fig. 3

G9 / D9

Dair-y Queen was on the scene, the Ev-'ry - Kid teen mag-a-zine, the Mo-tör-head and Mis-ter Clean, my pis-ton need-ed Valv-o-line.
Gi-ant squid, Ka - ra - te Kid, Sid Vi-cious and the kat-y-did; the Plan-et that we must For-bid, the Eng-lish Beat are in Ma-drid.

Gtr. 3

Chorus

Gtr. 1: w/ Riff B
Gtr. 3 tacet

G7 / C7 / G7 / C7

I will be your post-er child, _ ya know the world is ours for a lit-tle while. _ And then,

To Coda ⊕

G7 / C9 / G7

I will be your pos-ter child ___ to - night. ___ Ah,

Bridge

D9 / Bb / F/A / Gm / C

la, da, da, da, ba, _ ba, ba, dum. You got me on ___ this, well, and I can't get off ___

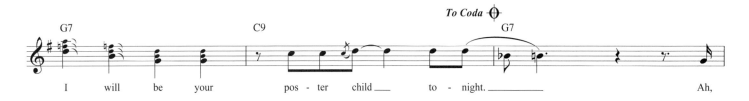

Rhy. Fill 2   End Rhy. Fill 2
Gtr. 1

w/ wah-wah   wah-wah off

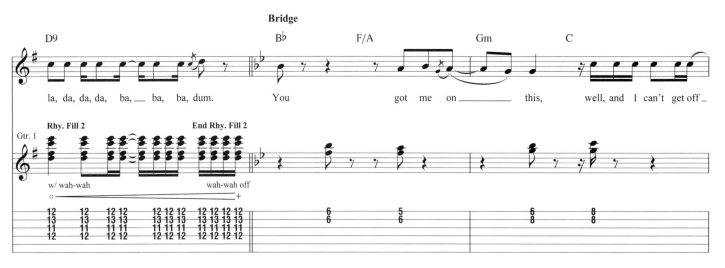

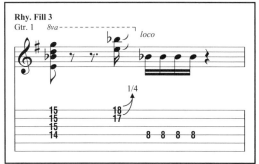

Rhy. Fill 3
Gtr. 1 *8va- - - - - - - - - - -*   *loco*

with no one else ____ but you. ____

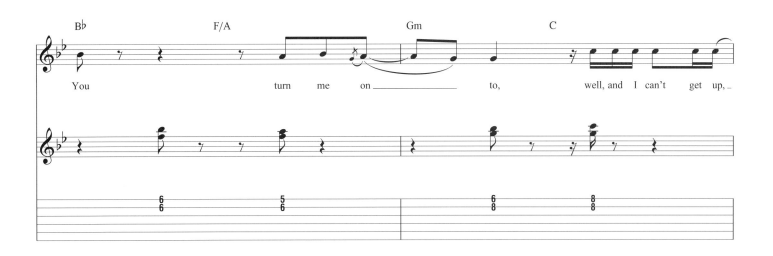

You ____ turn me on ____ to, ____ well, and I can't get up, ____

____ oo, ____ for no one else ____ but you. ____ 5. Cream

Verse

Gtr. 1: w/ Rhy. Fig. 1

Mag - a - zine, a Love Su - preme, the bal - lad of a Bil - lie Jean; and now we know the Sta - tus Quo, but God will nev - er Save the Queen.

Dave Mu-she-gain, Co-pen-ha-gen, cow-boy ghost of Ron-ald Rea-gan; dol-lar save was Fla-vo-Flav-in', cos-mic rays of Carl Sa-gan.

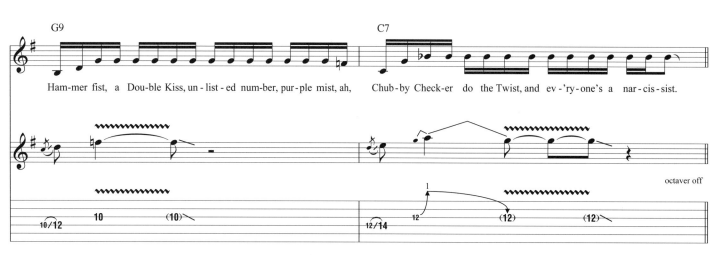

Ham-mer fist, a Dou-ble Kiss, un-list-ed num-ber, pur-ple mist, ah, Chub-by Check-er do the Twist, and ev-'ry-one's a nar-cis-sist.

Post-Verse

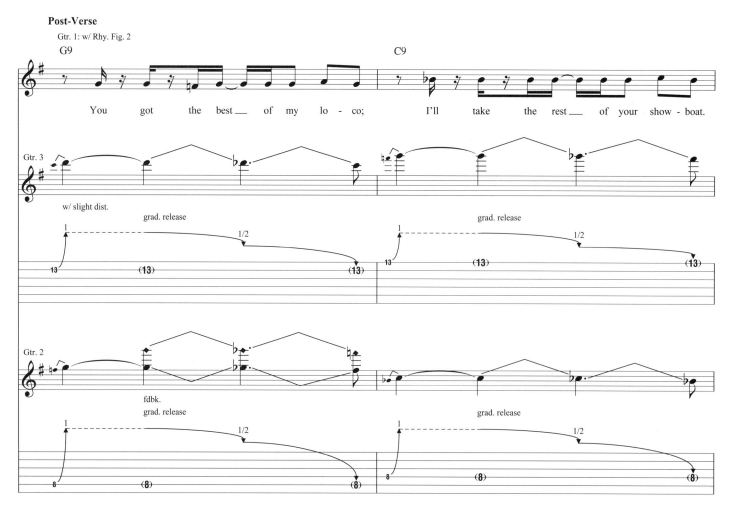

You got the best — of my lo-co; I'll take the rest — of your show-boat.

36

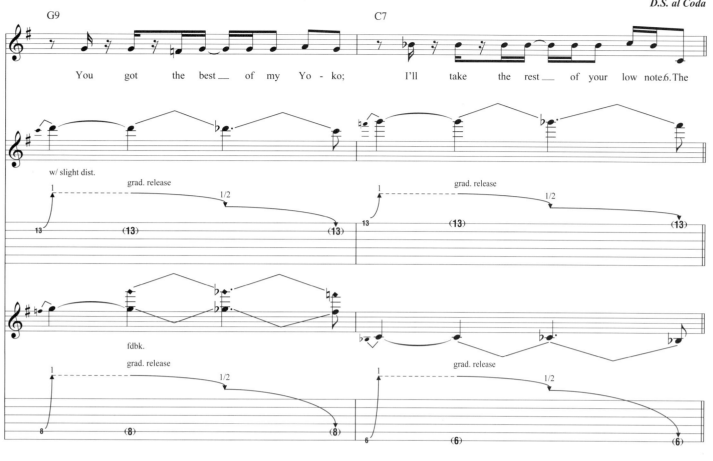

G9 / C7

You got the best __ of my Yo - ko; I'll take the rest __ of your low note. 6. The

w/ slight dist.

fdbk.

⊕ Coda

Gtr. 1: w/ Rhy. Fill 1

G7 / D9

La, da, da, da, ba, __ ba, ba, dum.

Chorus

Gtr. 1: w/ Riff B

G7 / C7 / G7 / C7

I will be your post - er child, __ ya know the world is ours for a lit - tle while. __ And then,

Gtr. 1: w/ Rhy. Fill 2

G7 / C9 / G7 / D9

I will be your pos - ter child __ to - night. __ La, da, da, da, ba, __ ba, ba, da, da.

Outro

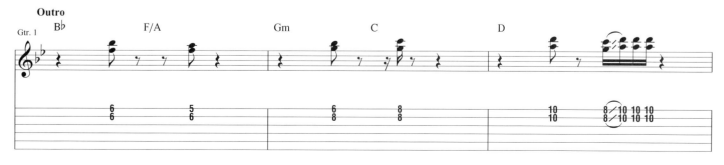

Gtr. 1

Bb / F/A / Gm / C / D

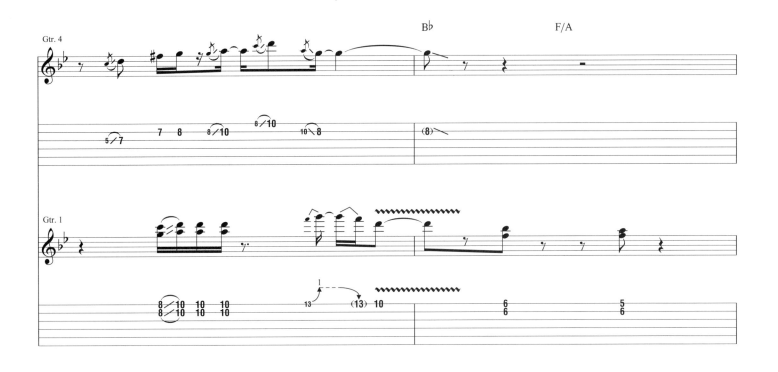

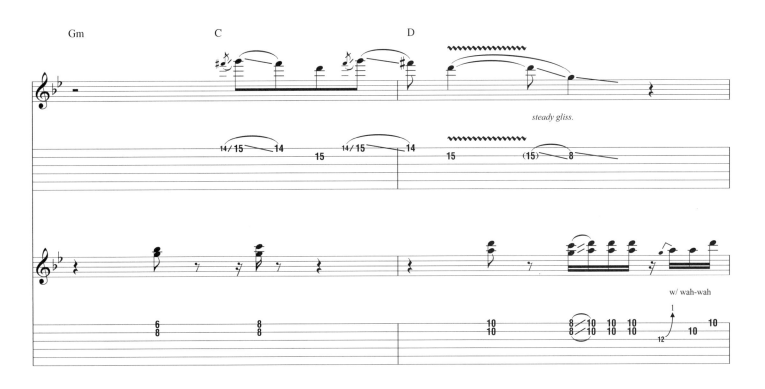

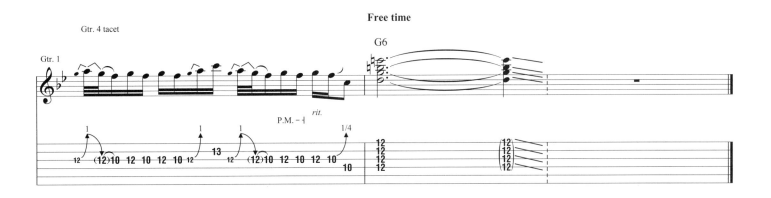

The Great Apes

Words and Music by Anthony Kiedis, Flea, Chad Smith and John Frusciante

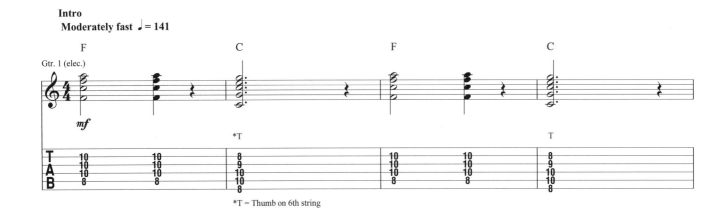

*T = Thumb on 6th string

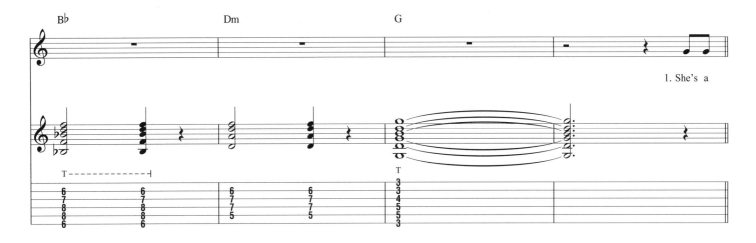

1. She's a

Verse

2nd time, Gtr. 2 tacet

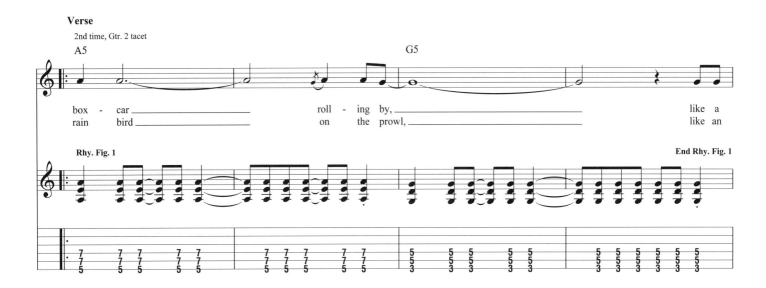

box - car _____ roll - ing by, _____ like a
rain bird _____ on the prowl, _____ like an

black star _____ in the sky. _____ She's a
urge to be your-self _____ that you won't al - low. _____ She's a

fail - ure _____ once or twice, _____ like a
for - est _____ that we burned, _____ just a

trail - er spin - ning out ____ up - on diz - zy ice. ____
blue - print for a life ____ that we nev - er learned. ____

Post-Verse

Gtr. 1 tacet

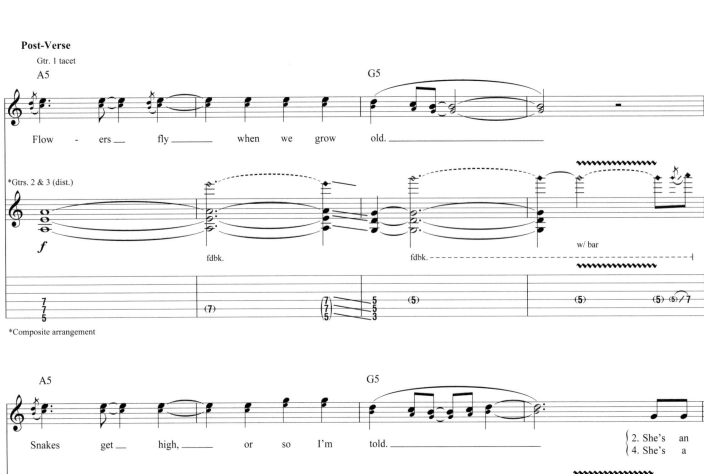

Flow-ers fly ___ when we grow old. ___

*Gtrs. 2 & 3 (dist.)

*Composite arrangement

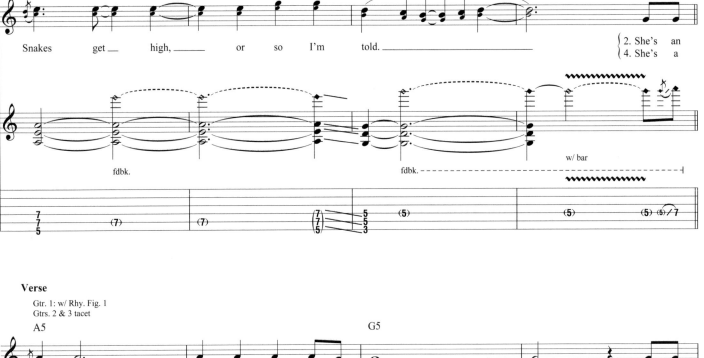

Snakes get ___ high, ___ or so I'm told. ___

2. She's an
4. She's a

Verse

Gtr. 1: w/ Rhy. Fig. 1
Gtrs. 2 & 3 tacet

ea - gle ___ out on the road,
lynch mob ___ on the street;

like my
take an -

fav - 'rite Bea - tle ev - 'ry-one bought and sold.
oth - er step and I ___ will kill the beat.

Gtr. 1

let ring ---

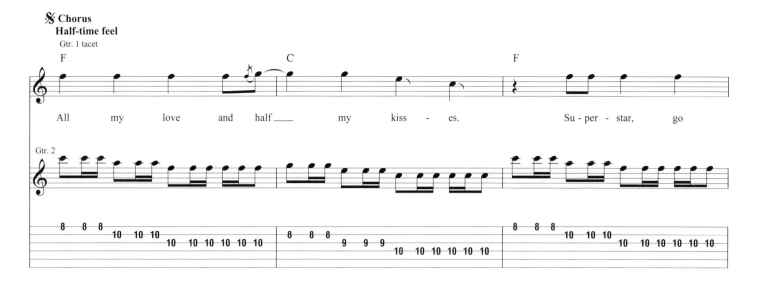

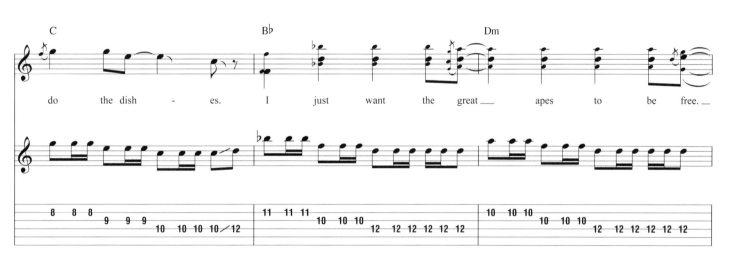

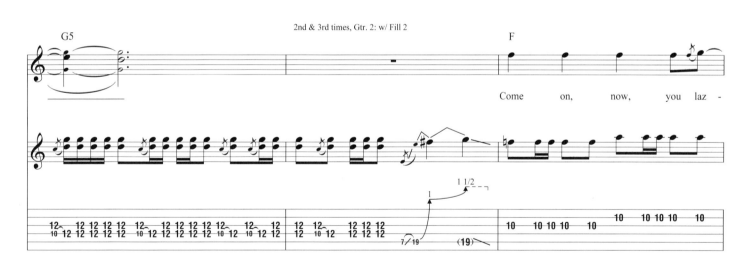

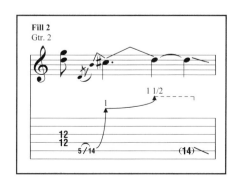

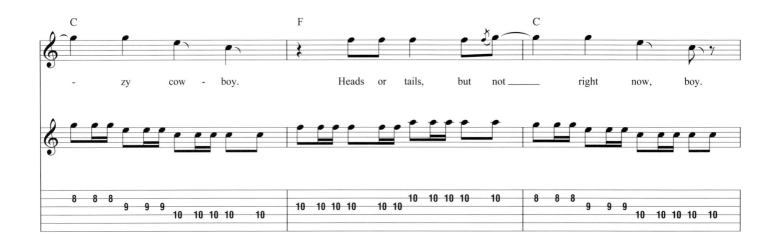

-zy cow - boy. Heads or tails, but not right now, boy.

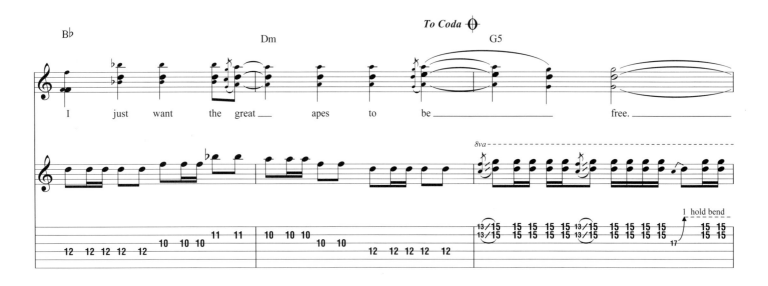

I just want the great apes to be free.

To Coda ⊕

1.

2.

End half-time feel

End half-time feel

3. She's a

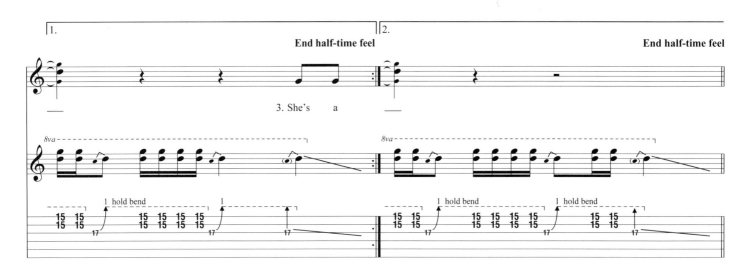

Guitar Solo

*A5

G5

*Chord symbols reflect overall harmony.

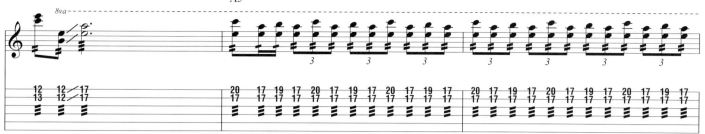

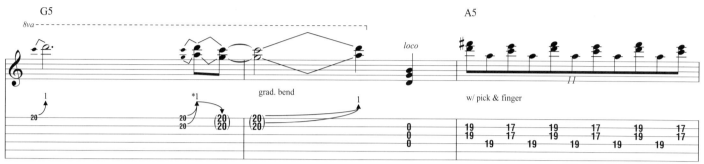

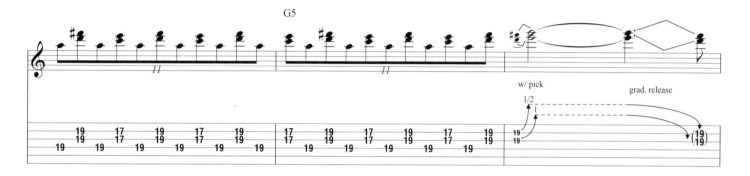

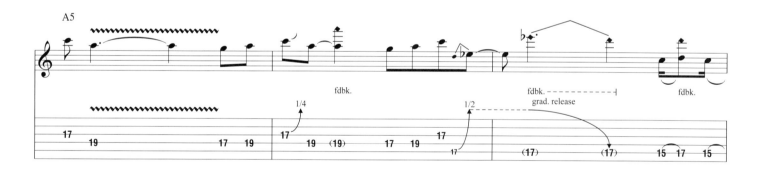

Verse

Gtr. 1: w/ Rhy. Fig. 1 (3 times)   Gtr. 2 tacet

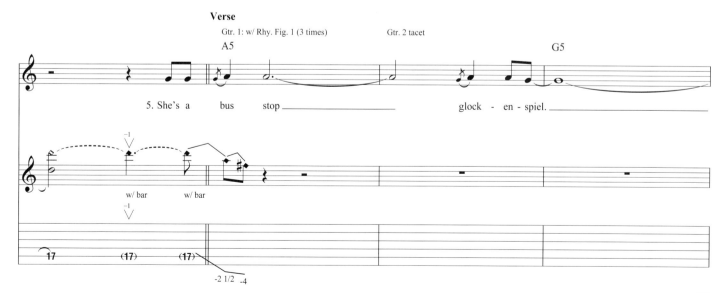

5. She's a bus stop _____ glock - en - spiel. _____

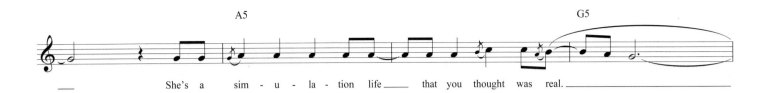

She's a sim - u - la - tion life___ that you thought was real.___

She's an im - age___ that we blurred.___ It's a

D.S. al Coda

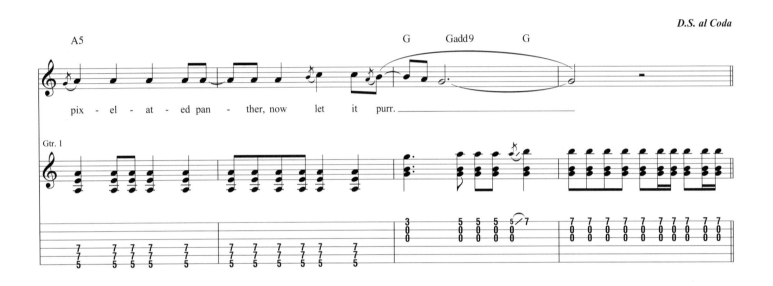

pix - el - at - ed pan - ther, now let it purr.___

Gtr. 1

⊕ Coda

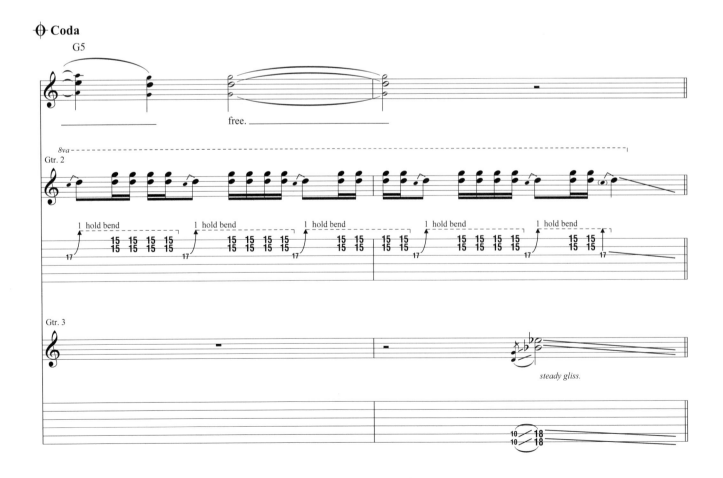

free.___

Gtr. 2

1 hold bend

Gtr. 3

steady gliss.

Outro-Chorus

*Chord symbols reflect combined harmony.

I just want the great apes to be free.

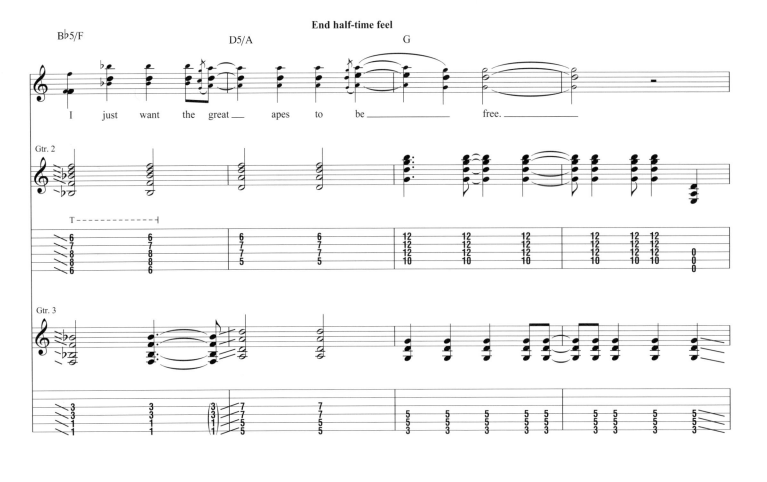

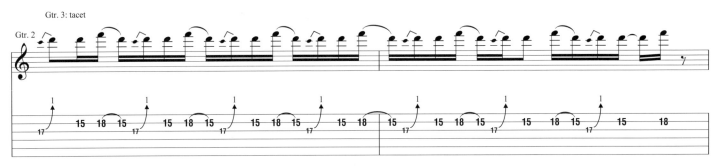

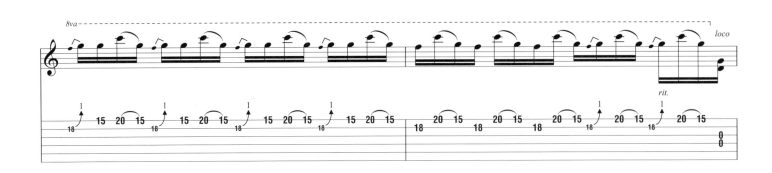

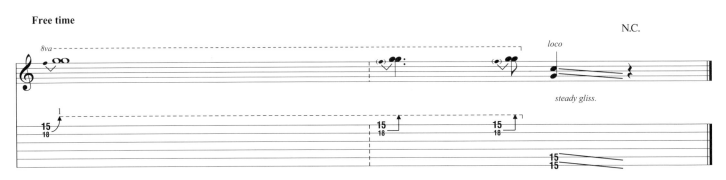

It's Only Natural

Words and Music by Anthony Kiedis, Flea, Chad Smith and John Frusciante

⅜ Chorus

2nd time, Gtr. 4 tacet

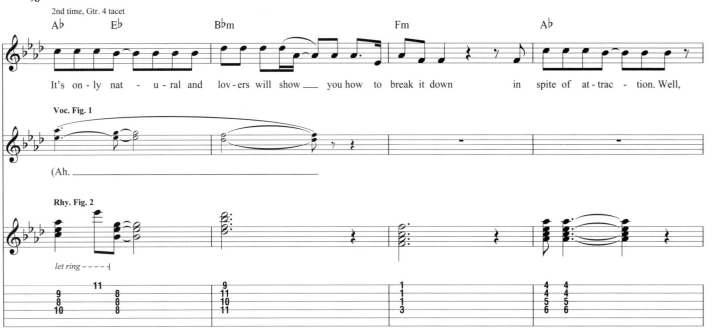

It's on-ly nat - u - ral and lov-ers will show ___ you how to break it down in spite of at - trac - tion. Well,

(Ah. _____

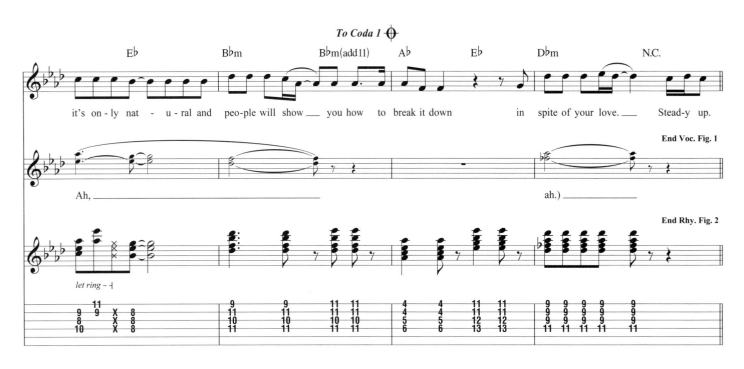

it's on-ly nat - u - ral and peo-ple will show ___ you how to break it down in spite of your love. ___ Stead-y up.

Ah, _____ ah.) _____

Interlude

Gtr. 1: w/ Rhy. Fig. 1 (2 times)

Gtr. 2 (clean)

Verse

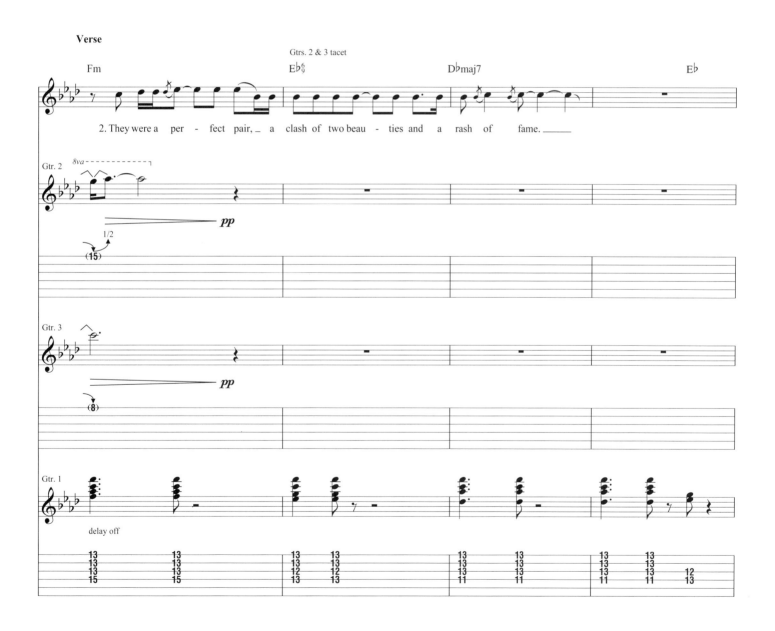

2. They were a per - fect pair, _ a clash of two beau - ties and a rash of fame. _____

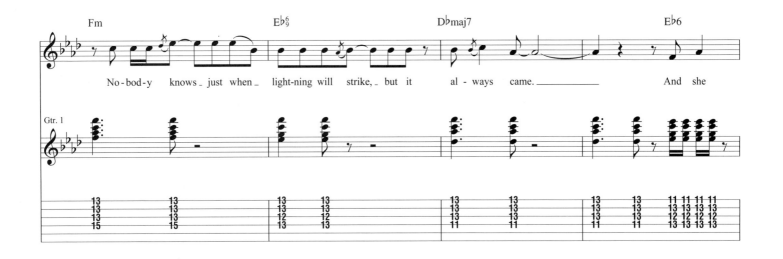

No-bod-y knows _ just when _ light-ning will strike, but it al-ways came. _____ And she

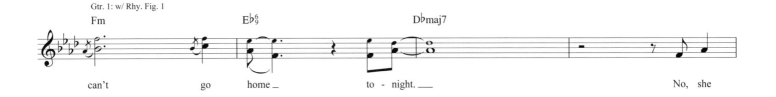

can't go home _ to - night. _____ No, she

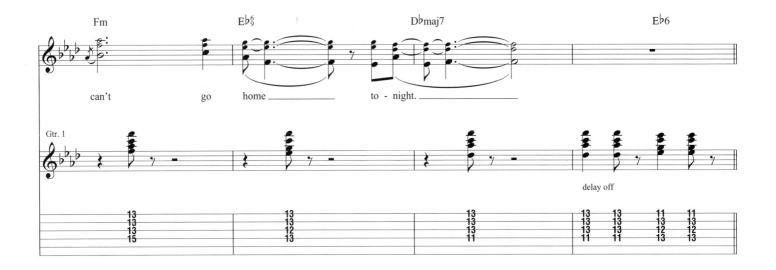

can't go home _____ to - night. _____

delay off

𝄋𝄋 Chorus

Bkgd. Voc.: w/ Voc. Fig. 1
Gtr. 1: w/ Rhy. Fig. 2

It's on - ly nat - u - ral and lov - ers will show _ you how to { break it down in spite of at - trac - tion. Well, / break it down. The per - fect sub - trac - tion. Well,

To Coda 2 ⊕

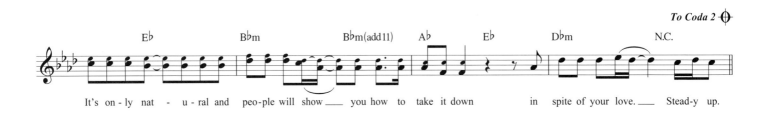

It's on - ly nat - u - ral and peo - ple will show _ you how to take it down in spite of your love. _ Stead-y up.

Guitar Solo

*Chord symbols reflect implied harmony.

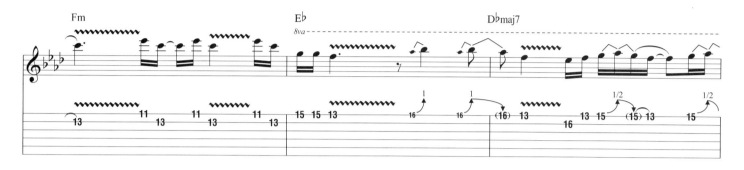

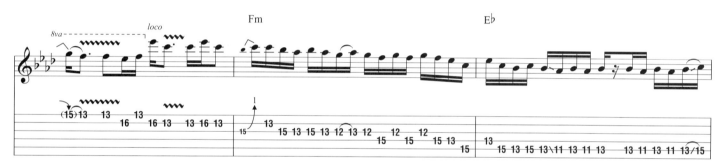

But she can't go

home to-night.

D.S. al Coda 1

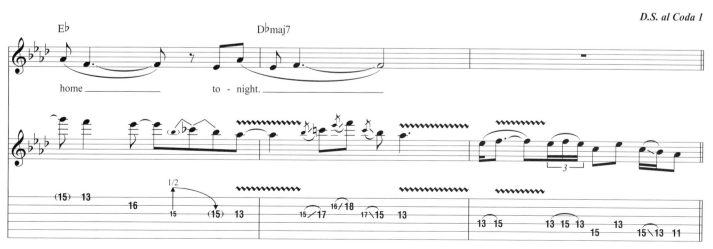

⊕ Coda 1

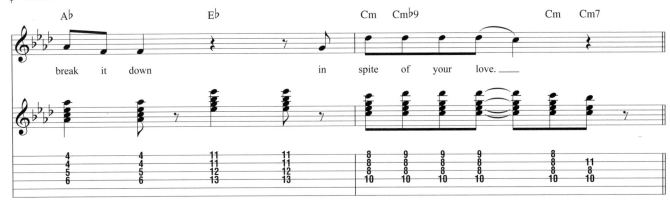

break it down   in spite of your love. ____

⊕ Coda 2

Outro

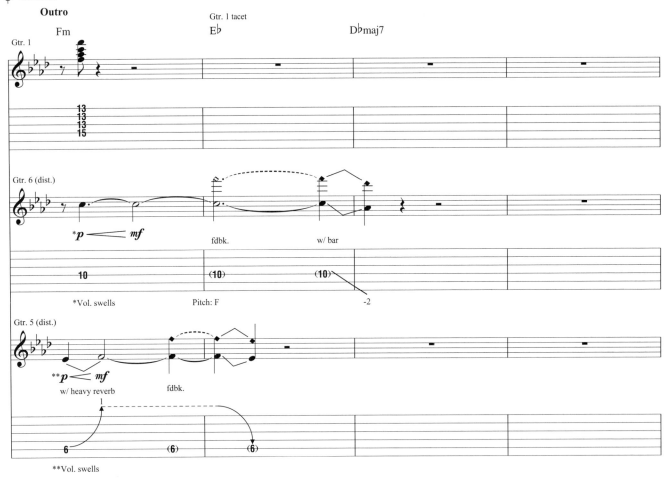

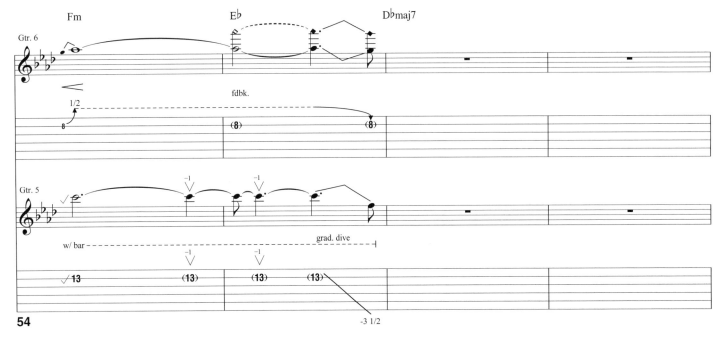

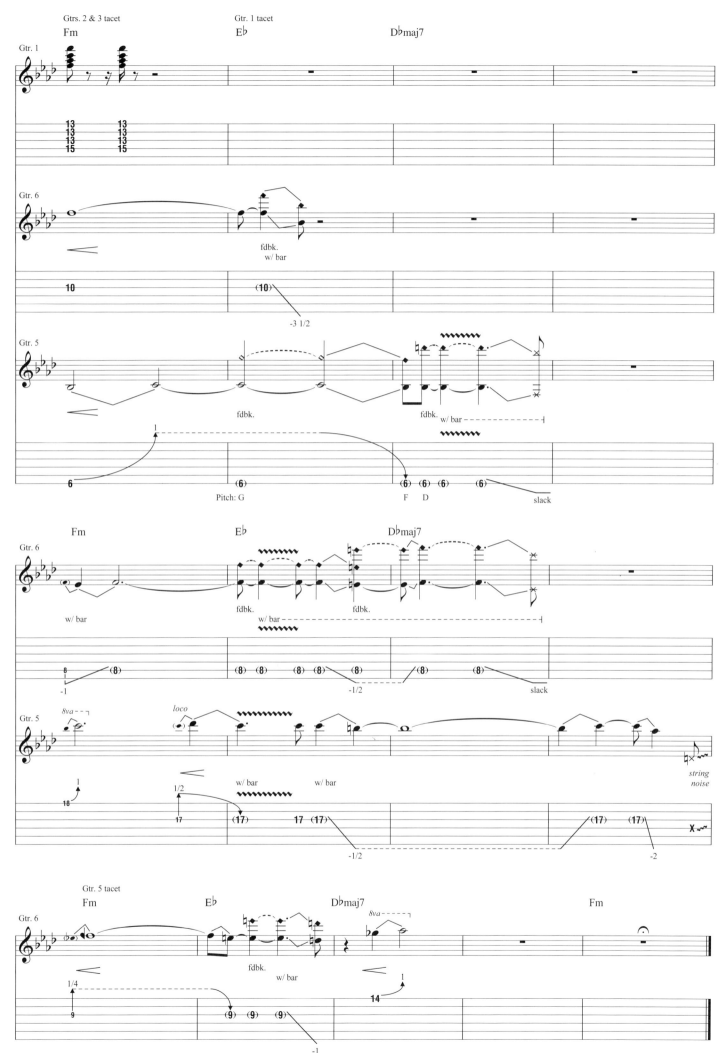

She's a Lover

Words and Music by Anthony Kiedis, Flea, Chad Smith and John Frusciante

*Chord symbols reflect implied harmony.

Verse lyrics:
1. The flow-er's pink on the tree. __ But if you pick it to see, __ will it be wild _ and free? __

You say you want-ed a piece. __ Is it for sale or for lease? __ Oh, that's the eas - y po - lice. __ Come on down.

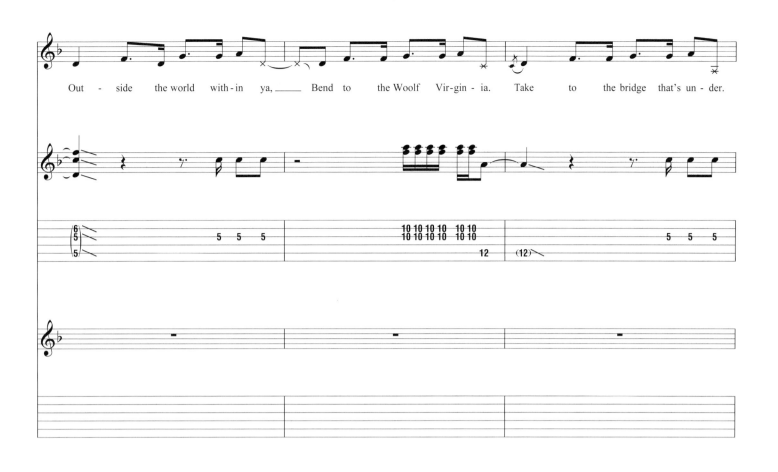

Out - side the world with - in ya, _____ Bend to the Woolf Vir - gin - ia. Take to the bridge that's un - der.

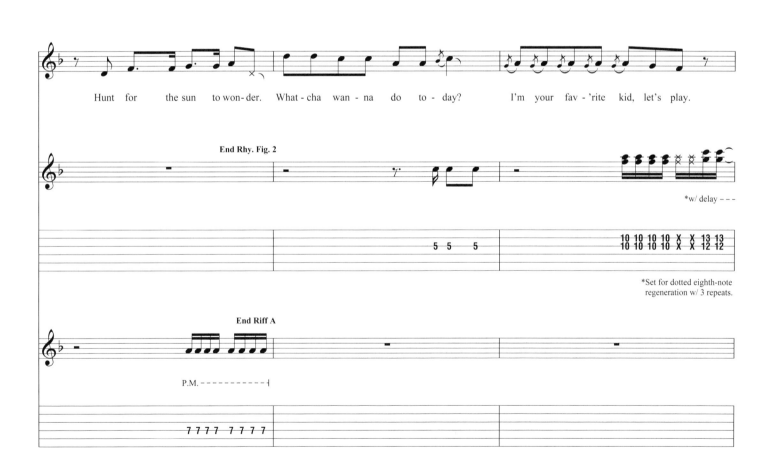

Hunt for the sun to won - der. What - cha wan - na do to - day? I'm your fav - 'rite kid, let's play.

End Rhy. Fig. 2

*w/ delay - - -

*Set for dotted eighth-note
regeneration w/ 3 repeats.

End Riff A

P.M. - - - - - - - - - - |

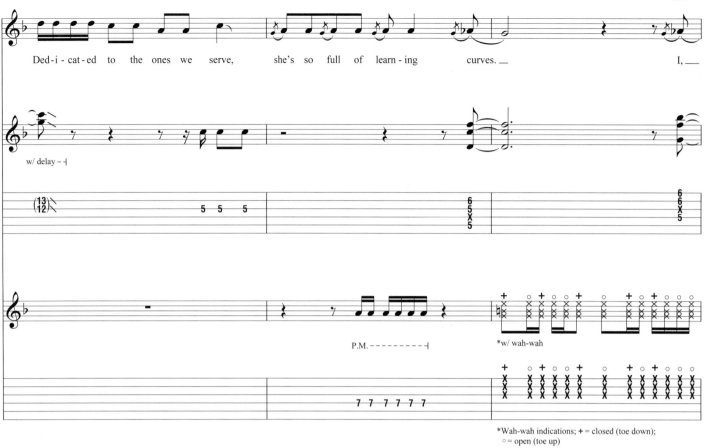

Ded-i-cat-ed to the ones we serve, she's so full of learn-ing curves. ___ I, ___

w/ delay

P.M. - - - - - - - -

*w/ wah-wah

*Wah-wah indications; + = closed (toe down);
○ = open (toe up)

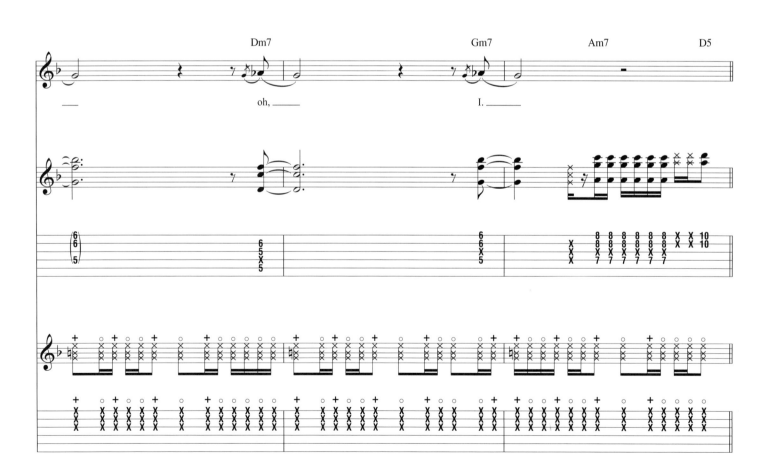

Dm7   Gm7   Am7   D5

___ oh, ___ I. ___

Coda

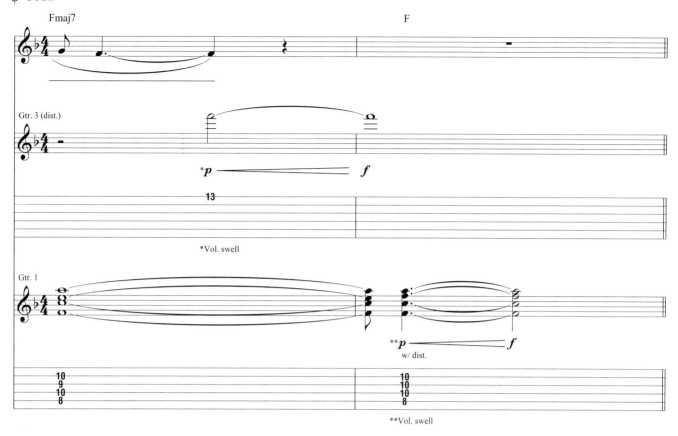

Guitar Solo

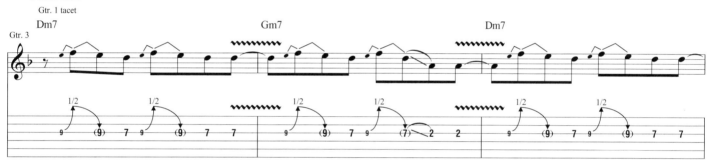

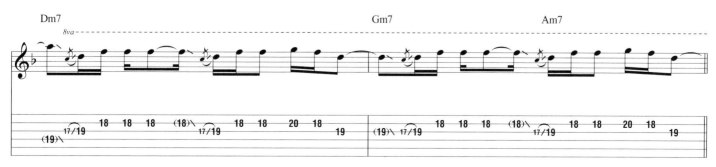

Outro-Chorus

*Gtr. 1: w/ Rhy. Fig. 4 (1st 6 meas.)

Love me, love me. Wake up and hug me. I will be a

*dist. off

tor-rid beast. Well, if you need me, need me, wake up and

Pitch: E

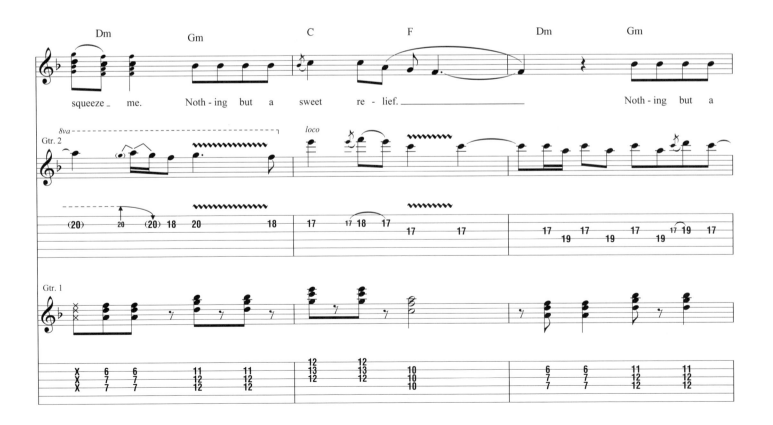

squeeze me. Noth-ing but a sweet re-lief. Noth-ing but a

These Are the Ways

Words and Music by Anthony Kiedis, Flea, Chad Smith and John Frusciante

*T = Thumb on 6th string

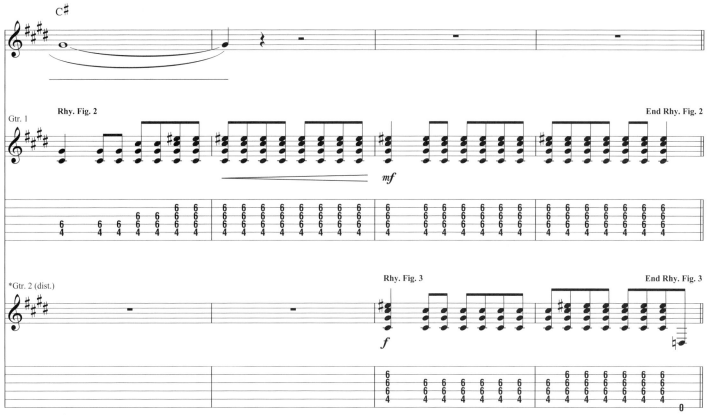

*Two gtrs. arr. for one.

%. Chorus

These are the ways when you come from A-mer-i-ca. The sights, the sounds the smells.

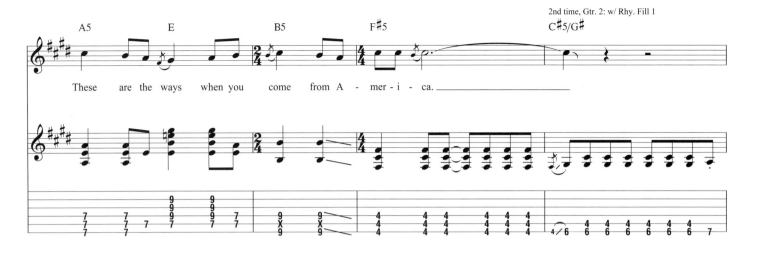

These are the ways when you come from A-mer-i-ca.

Half-time feel

I don't want to die and she's gon-na take good care of ya.

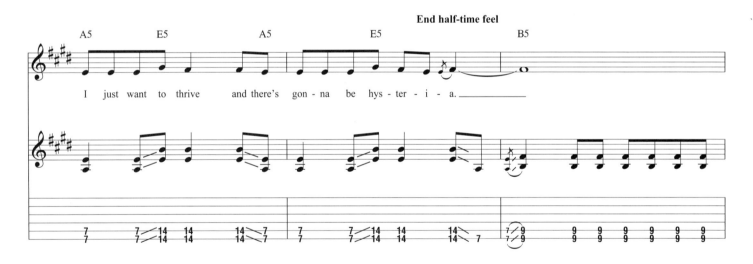

End half-time feel

I just want to thrive and there's gon-na be hys-ter-i-a.

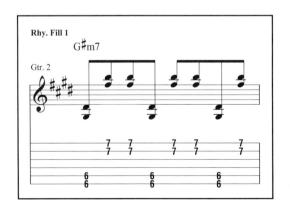

Rhy. Fill 1

G#m7

Gtr. 2

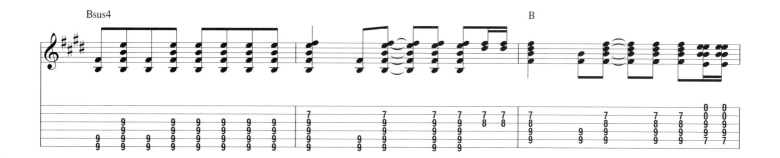

Bsus4 .... B

2nd time, Bkgd. Voc.: w/ Voc. Fig. 1

E5   F#7sus4   G6   Asus2

Don't   be   late.   Walk us   thru ___ the Gold - en Gate, _ yeah!

Rhy. Fig. 4   End Rhy. Fig. 4

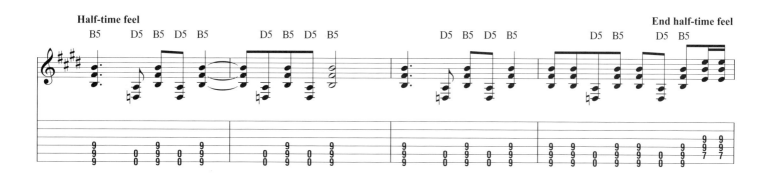

Half-time feel   End half-time feel

B5 D5 B5 D5 B5   D5 B5 D5 B5   D5 B5 D5 B5   D5 B5   D5 B5

To Coda ⊕

Gtr. 2: w/ Rhy. Fig. 4
2nd time, Bkgd. Voc.: w/ Voc. Fig. 1

E5   F#7sus4   G6   Asus2

Bruce   and   George   sing - ing   for ___ their own ___ re - ward. _

Voc. Fig. 1

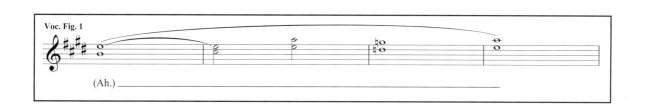

(Ah.) _____

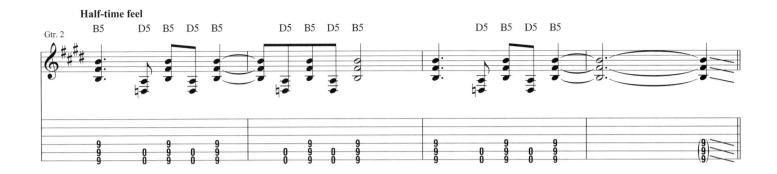

Verse

Gtr. 1: w/ Rhy. Fig. 1
Gtr. 2 tacet

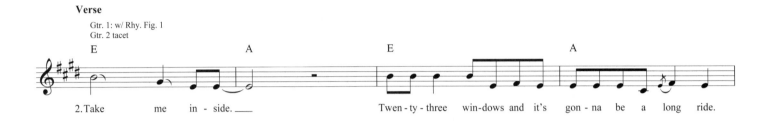

2.Take me in - side. ___ Twen - ty - three win - dows and it's gon - na be a long ride.

All had e - nough? ___ Have we all had too much? ___

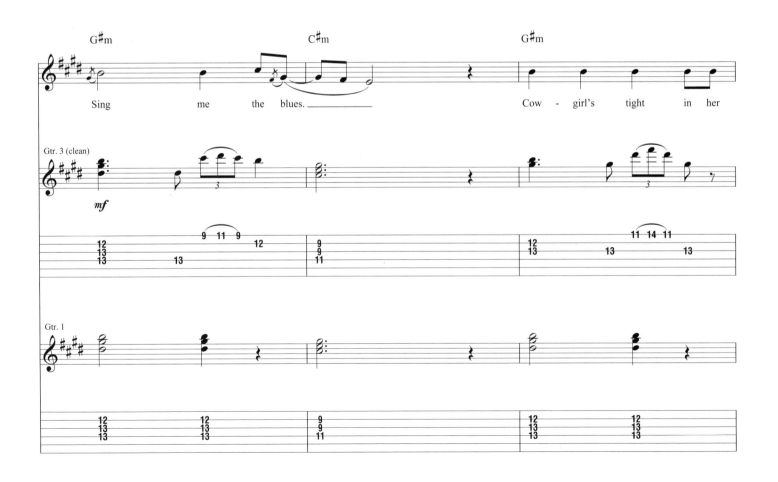

Sing me the blues. ___ Cow - girl's tight in her

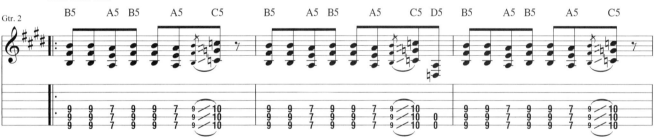

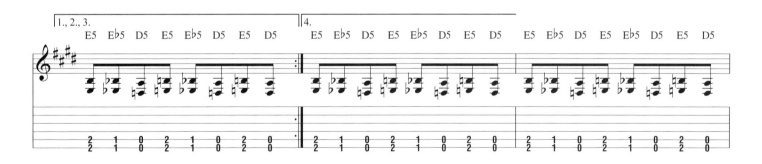

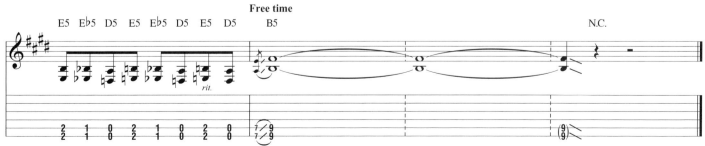

Whatchu Thinkin'

Words and Music by Anthony Kiedis, Flea, Chad Smith and John Frusciante

Intro
Moderately slow ♩ = 86

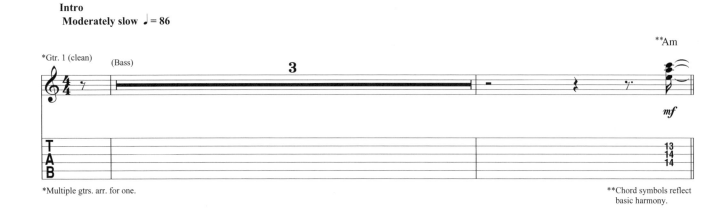

*Gtr. 1 (clean)   (Bass)

*Multiple gtrs. arr. for one.

**Am

**Chord symbols reflect basic harmony.

Verse

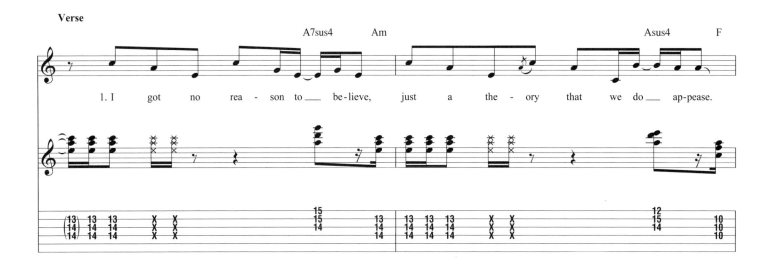

A7sus4   Am   Asus4   F

1. I got no rea - son to __ be - lieve, just a the - o - ry that we do __ ap-pease.

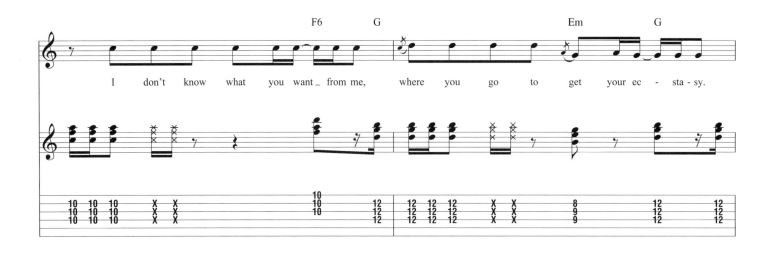

F6   G   Em   G

I don't know what you want __ from me, where you go to get your ec - sta - sy.

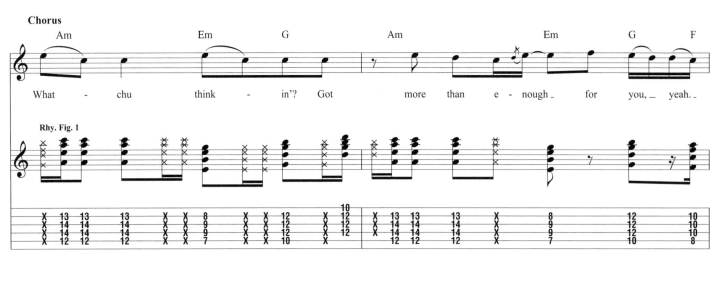

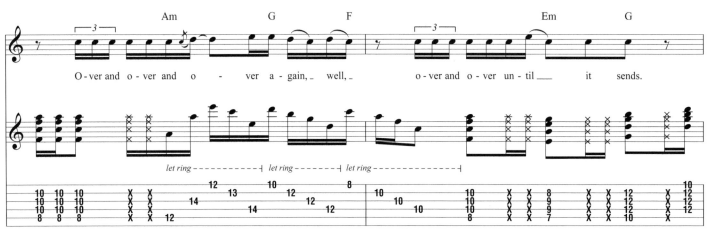

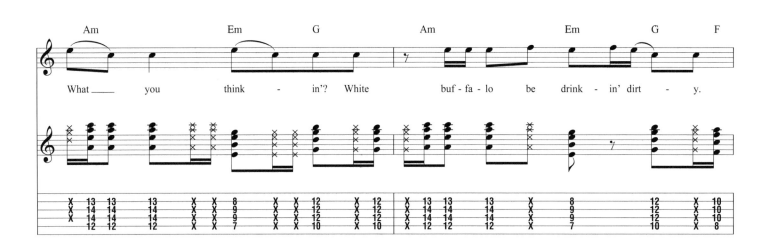

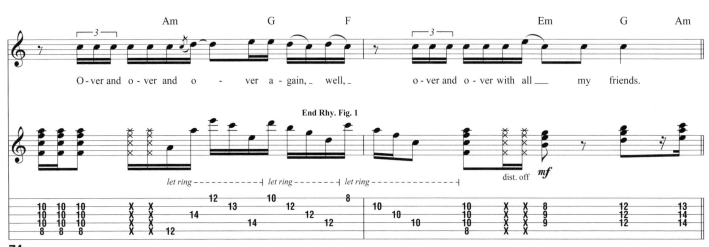

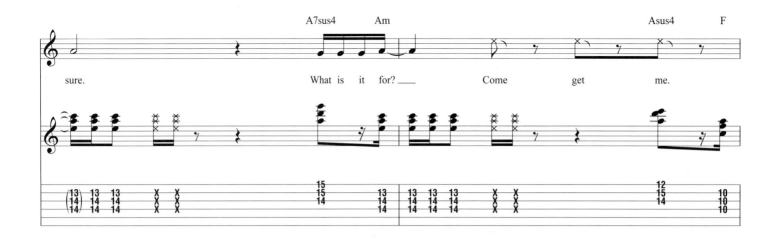

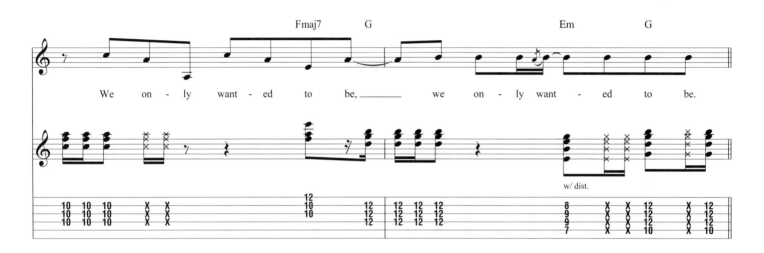

Chorus

Gtr. 1: w/ Rhy. Fig. 1 (1st 6 meas.)

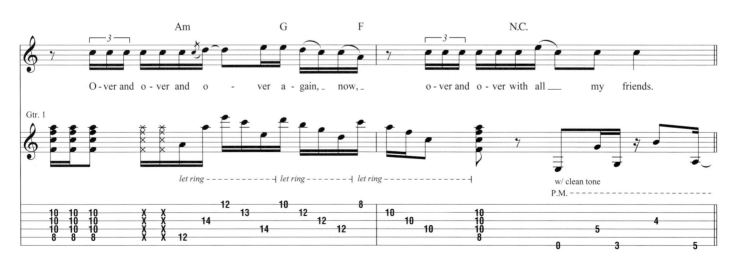

Chorus

Gtr. 1: w/ Rhy. Fig. 1 (1st 6 meas.)

What-chu think-in'? Got more than e-nough __ for you, __ well. __

O-ver and o-ver and o- ver a-gain, yeah, __ o-ver and o-ver un-til ___ it sends.

What ___ you think - in'? White buf-fa-lo be drink-in' dirt - y.

O-ver and o-ver and o- ver a-gain, __ now, __ o-ver and o-ver with all ___ my friends.

Gtr. 2 (dist.)

Gtr. 1

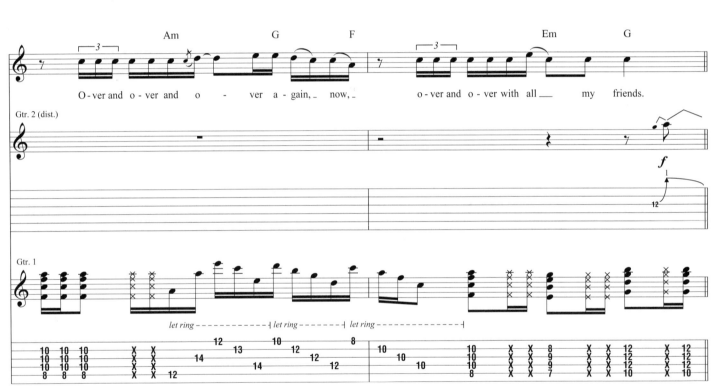

Outro-Guitar Solo

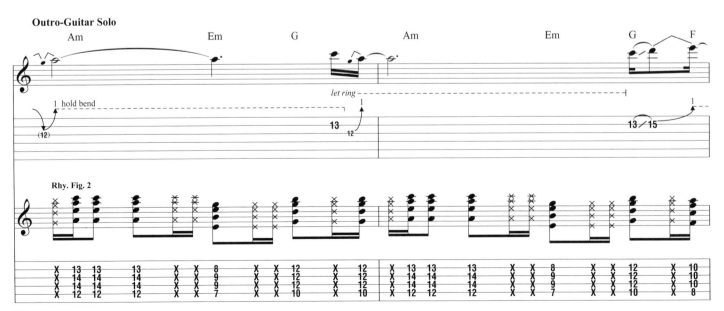

Rhy. Fig. 2

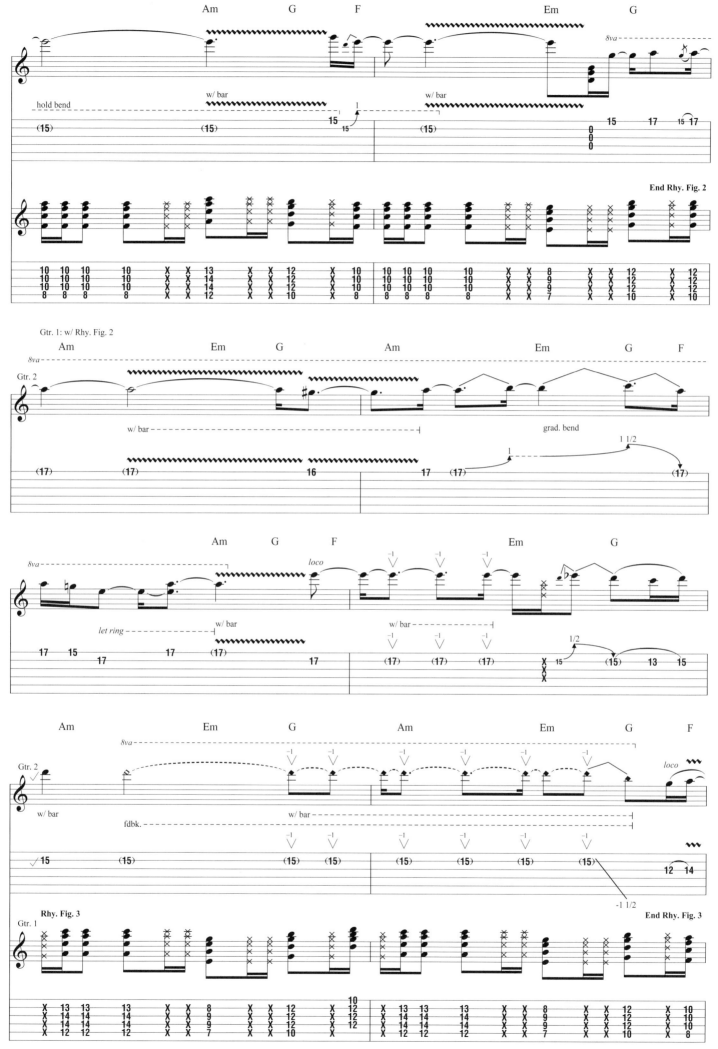

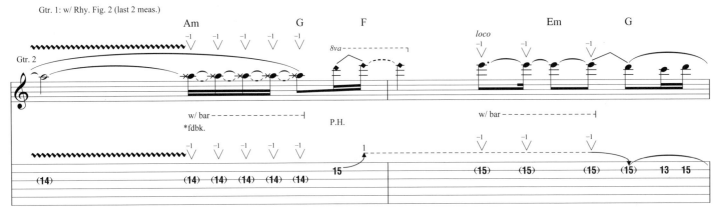

*Microphonic fdbk., not caused by string vibration.

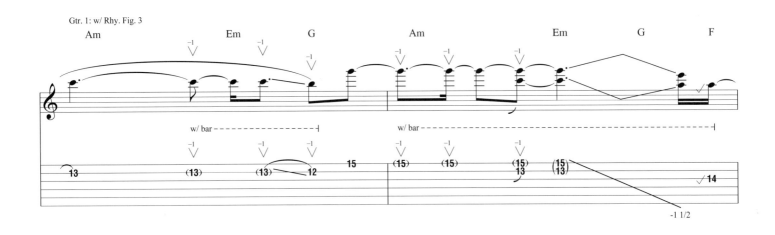

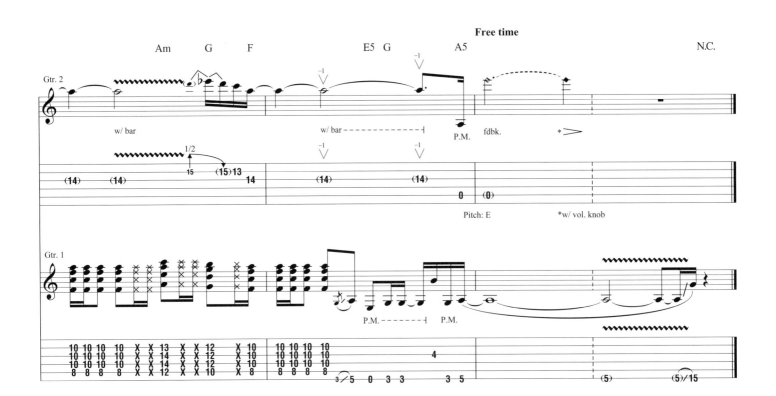

Bastards of Light

Words and Music by Anthony Kiedis, Flea, Chad Smith and John Frusciante

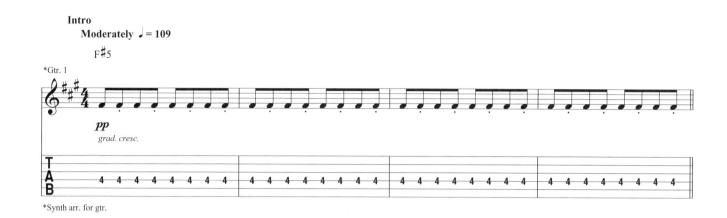

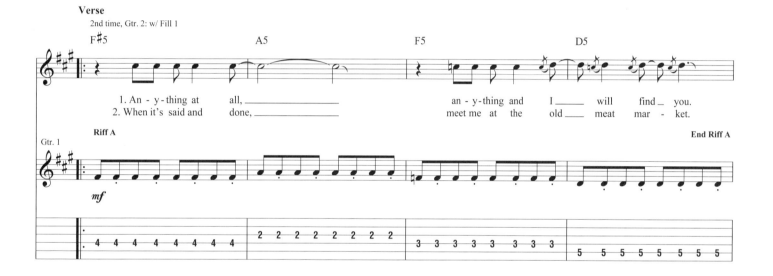

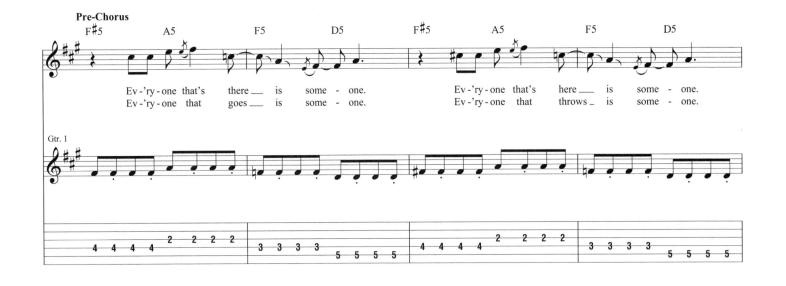

Ev-'ry-one that's there ___ is some - one.
Ev-'ry-one that goes ___ is some - one.
Ev-'ry-one that's here ___ is some - one.
Ev-'ry-one that throws ___ is some - one.

2nd time, Gtr. 3: w/ Rhy. Fill 1

Ev-'ry-one, I swear, ___ is some - one's daugh - ter. ___
Ev-'ry-one that knows, ___ it's in ___ the wat - er. ___

And it feels ___

Gtr. 2 (elec.)

mf
w/ slight dist.
w/ slide

Gtr. 1

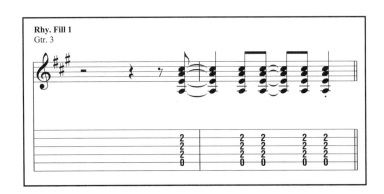

Rhy. Fill 1
Gtr. 3

*Two gtrs. arr. for one.

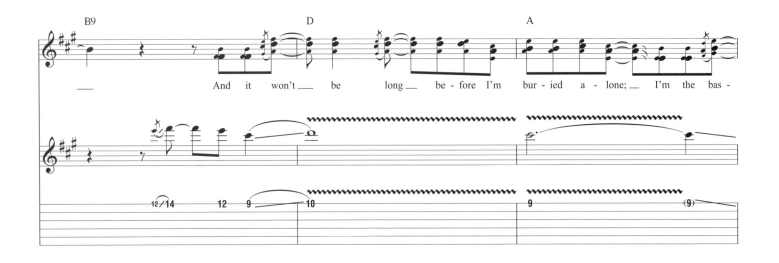

And it won't ___ be long ___ be - fore I'm bur - ied a - lone; ___ I'm the bas -

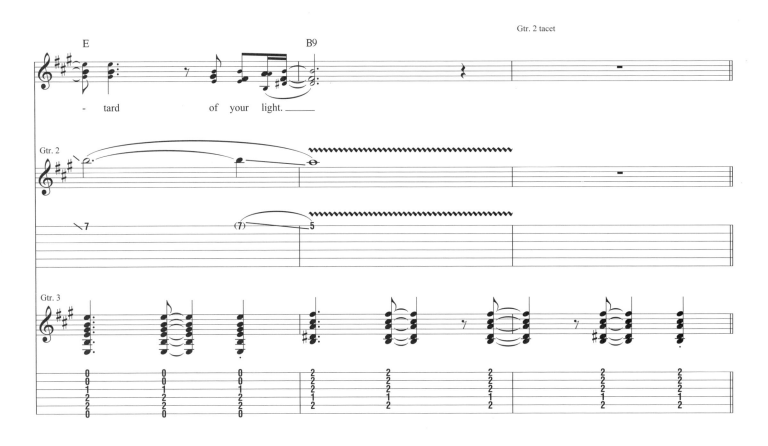

- tard of your light. ___

Gtr. 2 tacet

Gtr. 2

Gtr. 3

Bridge

Gtr. 3 tacet

F#5   A5   N.C.   F#5 A5 C5   B5   F#5   A5   N.C.   F   C5   E5

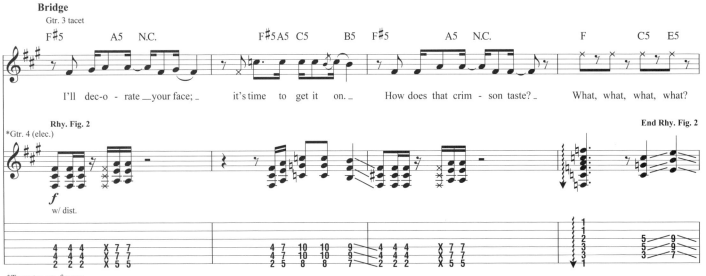

I'll dec-o - rate ___ your face; ___   it's time to get it   on. ___   How does that crim - son taste? _   What, what, what, what?

Rhy. Fig. 2   End Rhy. Fig. 2

*Gtr. 4 (elec.)

f
w/ dist.

*Two gtrs. arr. for one.

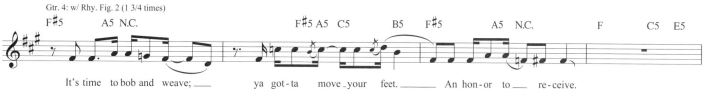

It's time to bob and weave; ___ ya got-ta move ___ your feet. ___ An hon-or to re-ceive.

To - ma - to cans ___ on tap, an - oth - er dan - dy chap. _ How 'bout a can - vas nap?

One, two, three, four! And it

Chorus

feels so ___ good up-on a Sat-ur-day night, ___ when the bas - tards come ___ to fight. ___ And it won't ___

*w/ sporadic tremolo till end.

___ be long ___ be-fore they car - ry me home; ___ I'm the bas - tard of your light. ___ And it feels ___

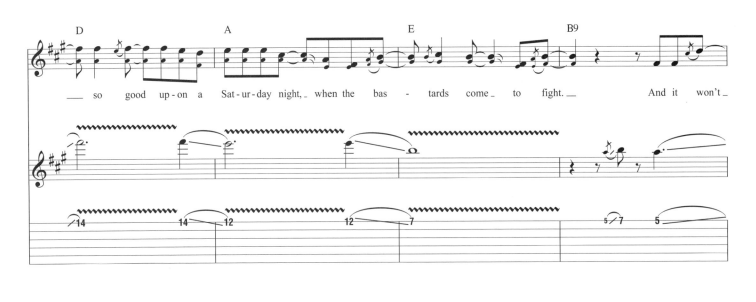

so good up-on a Sat-ur-day night, when the bas - tards come to fight. And it won't

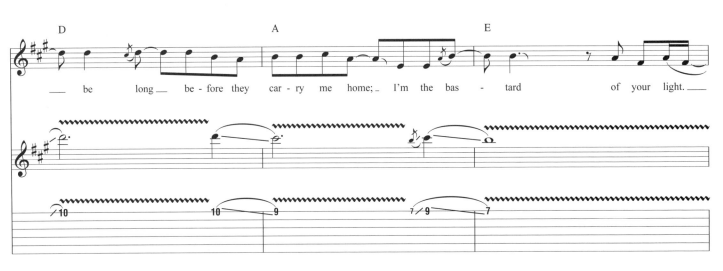

be long be-fore they car - ry me home; I'm the bas - tard of your light.

Free time

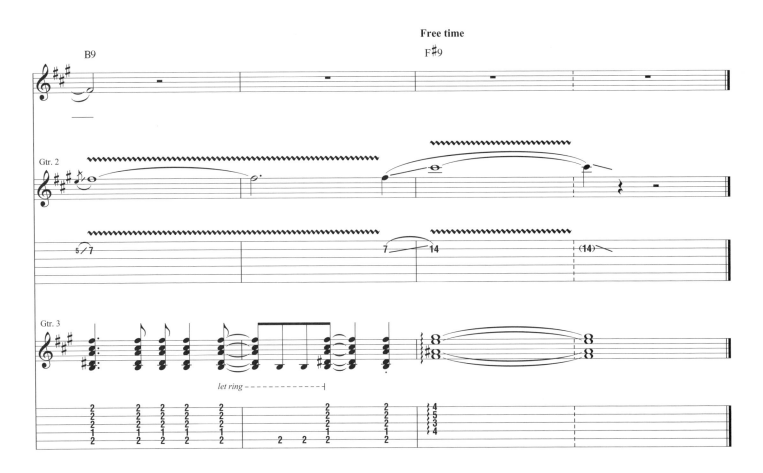

White Braids & Pillow Chair

Words and Music by Anthony Kiedis, Flea, Chad Smith and John Frusciante

Intro
Moderately ♩ = 108

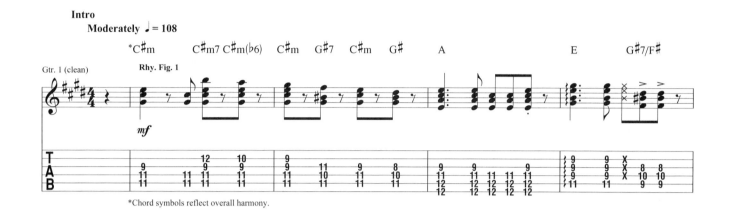

*Chord symbols reflect overall harmony.

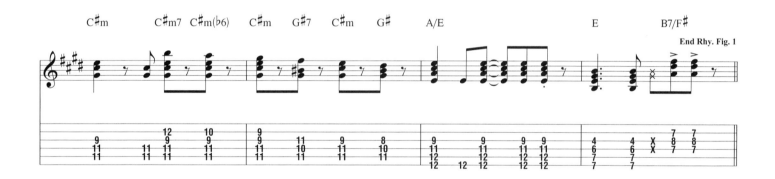

Verse

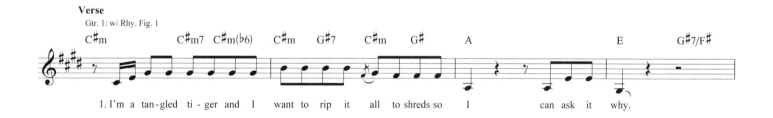

1. I'm a tan-gled ti-ger and I want to rip it all to shreds so I can ask it why.

She's a load-ed co-bra and she want-ed to be with me for the ride.

In a Sun-day din-er, I'm re-mind-ed there's no fin-er place to kiss than one like this. But

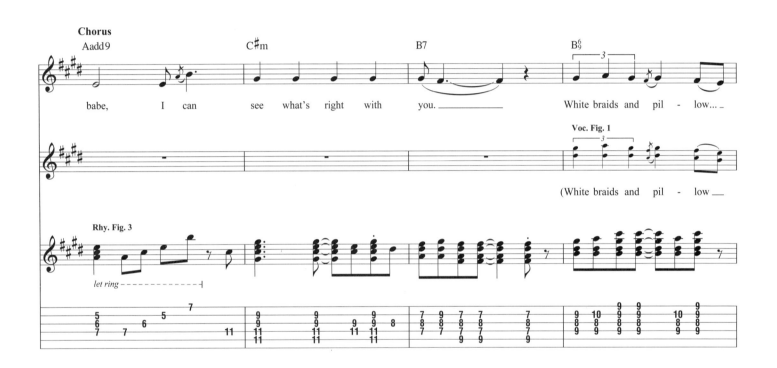

Chorus

babe, I can see what's right with you. ___ White braids and pil - low... _

(White braids and pil - low _

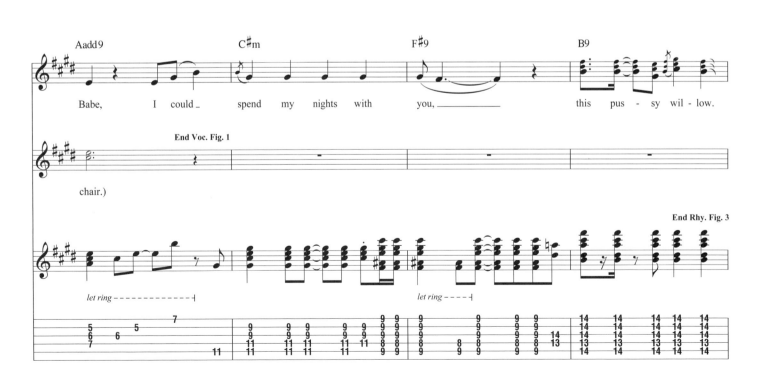

Babe, I could _ spend my nights with you, ___ this pus-sy wil-low.

chair.)

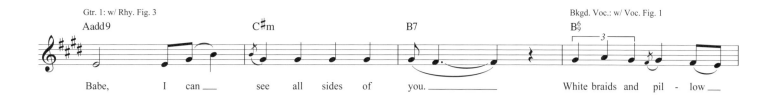

Gtr. 1: w/ Rhy. Fig. 3

Bkgd. Voc.: w/ Voc. Fig. 1

Aadd9   C#m   B7   B9⁶

Babe, I can __ see all sides of you. __ White braids and pil - low __

Aadd9   C#m   F#9   B9

chair. I don't know what I would do __ with - out __ your pil - low.

Verse

Gtr. 1: w/ Rhy. Fig. 1

C#m   C#m7 C#m(♭6)   C#m G#7   C#m   G#   A   E   G#7/F#

2. She's a Bob - by Dar - in sing - ing to the fish and her - ring sac - ri - fice. __ Ah, that's her knife.

C#m   C#m7 C#m(♭6)   C#m G#7   C#m   G#   A/E   E   B7/F#

There's a Kar - mann Ghi - a parked out back and we be - lieve it is a - live, _____ oh.

Gtr. 1: w/ Rhy. Fig. 2

C#m   C#m7 C#m(♭6)   C#m G#7   C#m   G#   A   E   B7/F#

You can see the riv - er run - ning through my dev - as - tat - ed con - crete eyes. They don't de - ny. But

Chorus

Gtr. 1: w/ Rhy. Fig. 3 (1 3/4 times)

Bkgd. Voc.: w/ Voc. Fig. 1

Aadd9   C#m   B7   B9⁶

babe, I can see what's right with you. _____ White braids and pil - low... __

Voc. Fig. 2

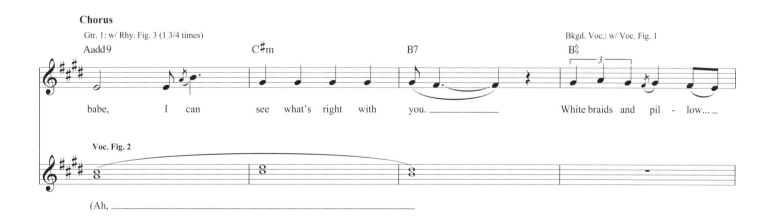

(Ah, _____

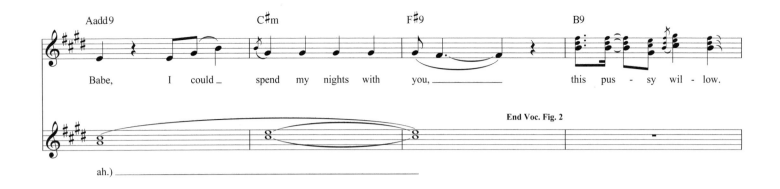

Babe, I could__ spend my nights with you,_____ this pus-sy wil-low.

ah.)

End Voc. Fig. 2

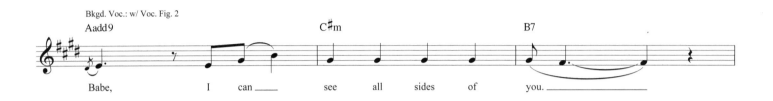

Bkgd. Voc.: w/ Voc. Fig. 2

Babe, I can__ see all sides of you._____

Bkgd. Voc.: w/ Voc. Fig. 1

White braids and pil - low... __ Babe, I don't know what I would

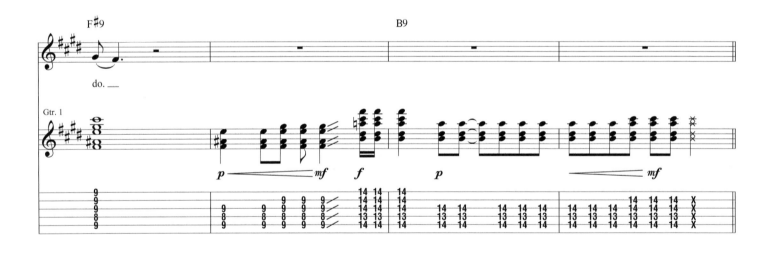

do. __

Gtr. 1

p — *mf* *f* *p* — *mf*

Outro
Double-time feel

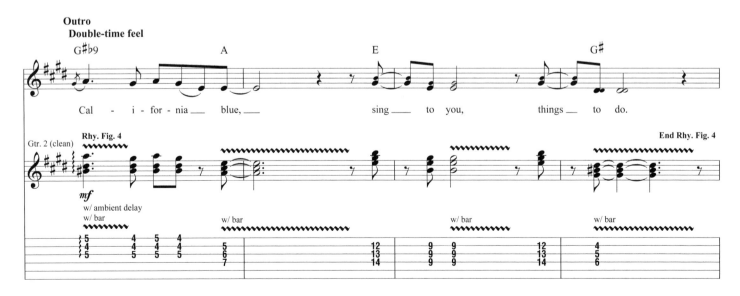

Cal - i-for-nia __ blue, __ sing __ to you, things __ to do.

Gtr. 2 (clean)

Rhy. Fig. 4

mf
w/ ambient delay
w/ bar

w/ bar

w/ bar

w/ bar

End Rhy. Fig. 4

One Way Traffic

Words and Music by Anthony Kiedis, Flea, Chad Smith and John Frusciante

*Chord symbols reflect overall harmony.

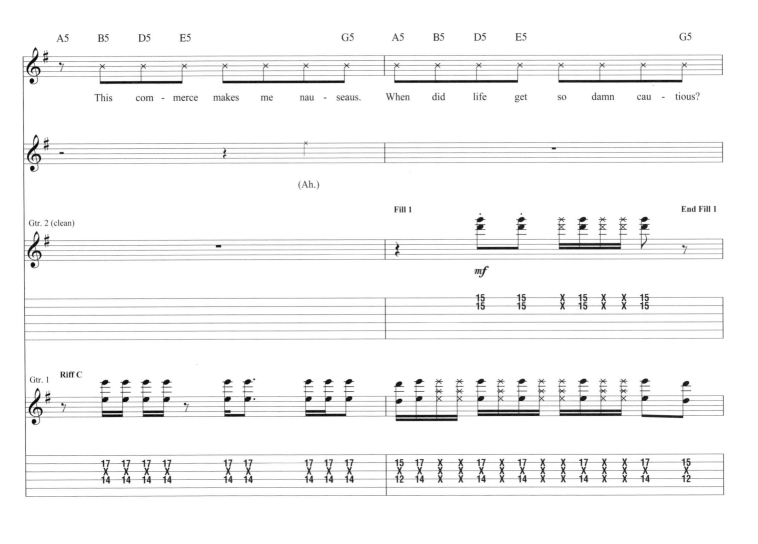

This com - merce makes me nau - seaus. When did life get so damn cau - tious?

(Ah.)

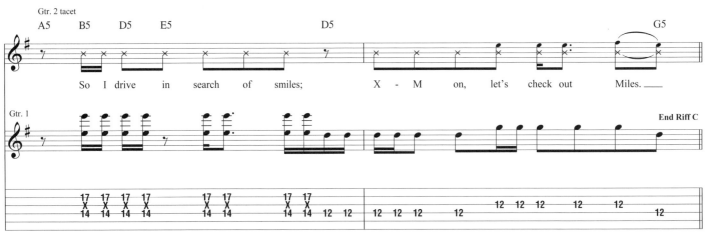

So I drive in search of smiles; X - M on, let's check out Miles.

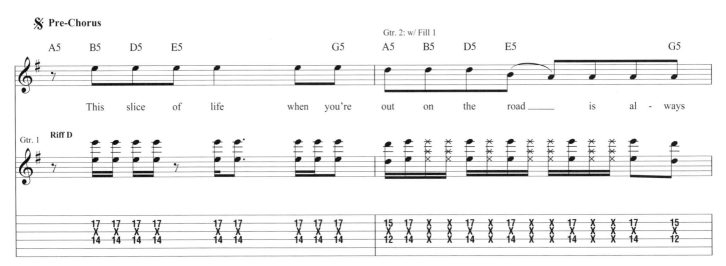

𝄋 Pre-Chorus

This slice of life when you're out on the road is al - ways

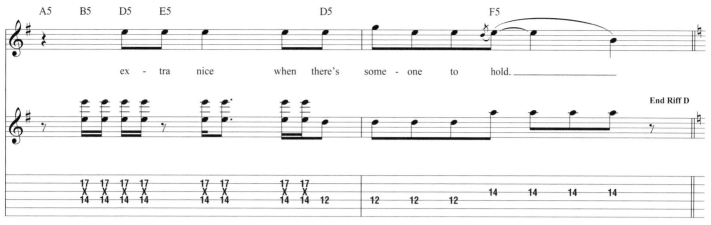

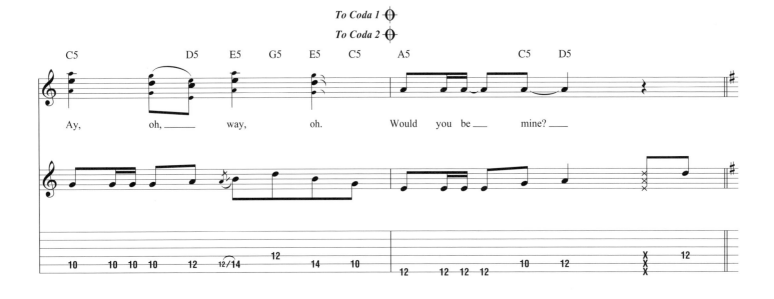

To Coda 1
To Coda 2

Ay, oh, way, oh. Would you be mine?

Verse

Gtr. 1: w/ Riff A

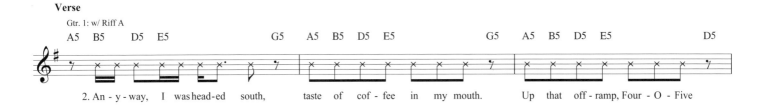

2. An-y-way, I was head-ed south, taste of cof-fee in my mouth. Up that off-ramp, Four-O-Five

Gtr. 1: w/ Riff B

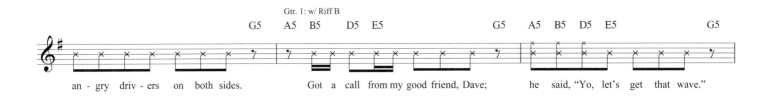

an-gry driv-ers on both sides. Got a call from my good friend, Dave; he said, "Yo, let's get that wave."

Gtr. 1: w/ Riff C

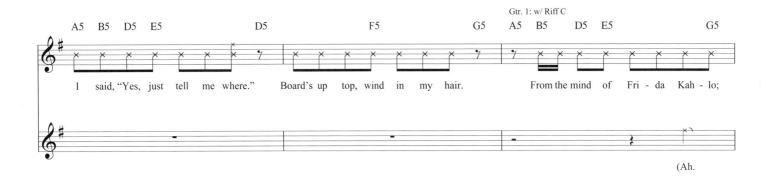

I said, "Yes, just tell me where." Board's up top, wind in my hair. From the mind of Fri-da Kah-lo;

(Ah.

D.S. al Coda 1

Gtr. 2: w/ Fill 1

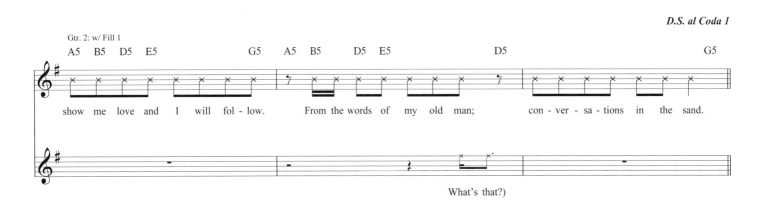

show me love and I will fol-low. From the words of my old man; con-ver-sa-tions in the sand.

What's that?)

Coda 1

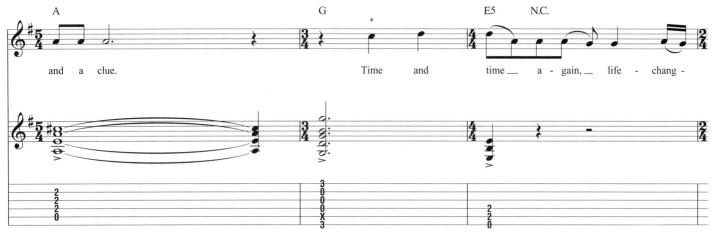

*w/ echo set for quarter-note regeneration w/ 2 repeats, next 2 meas.

Tempo I

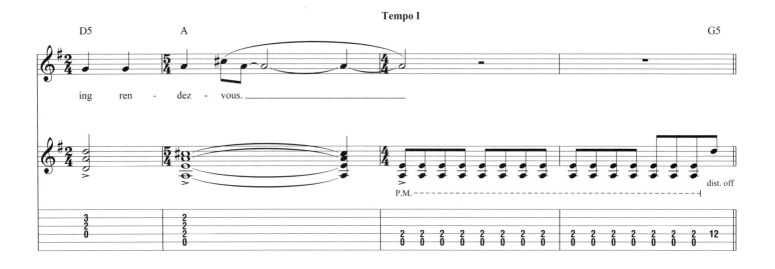

Verse

Gtr. 1: w/ Riff C

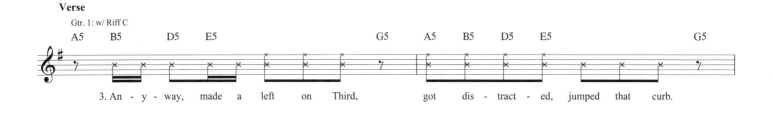

3. An - y - way, made a left on Third, got dis - tract - ed, jumped that curb.

Gtr. 1: w/ Riff B

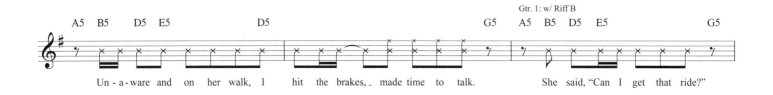

Un - a - ware and on her walk, I hit the brakes, made time to talk. She said, "Can I get that ride?"

"Oh, my God, just get in - side." It was all that I im - ag - ined, born to ride, en - thu - si - as - m.

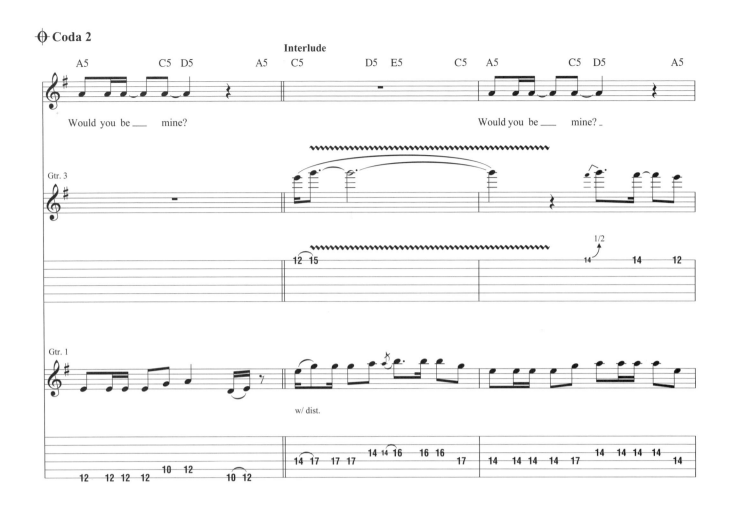

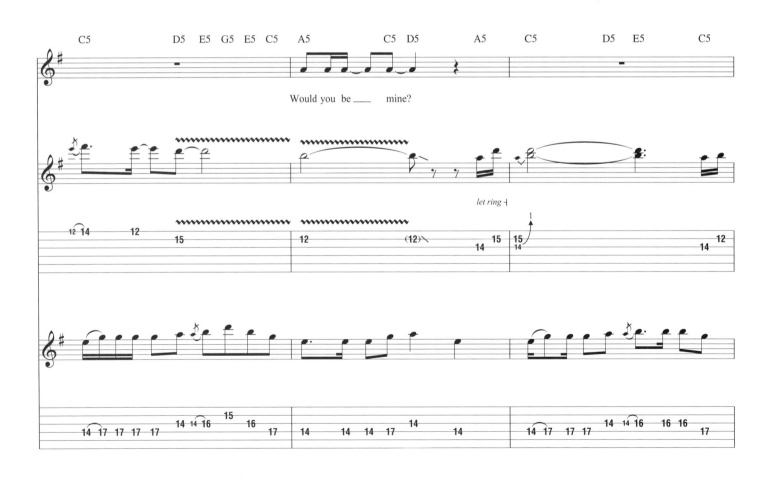

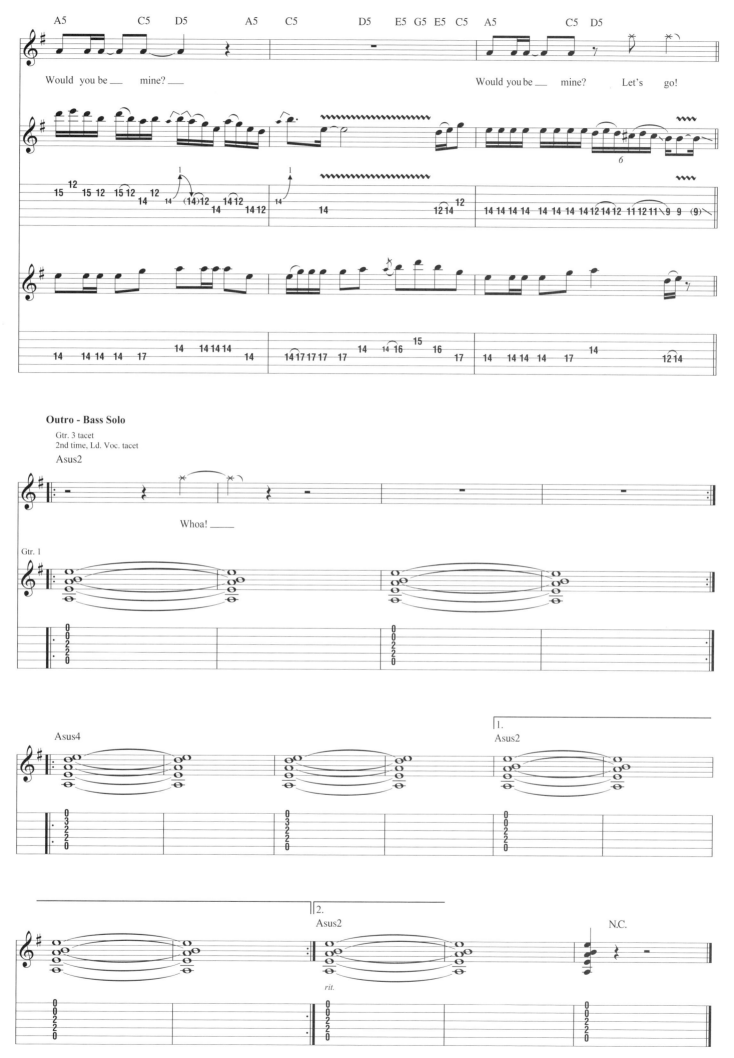

Outro - Bass Solo

Gtr. 3 tacet
2nd time, Ld. Voc. tacet

Veronica

Words and Music by Anthony Kiedis, Flea, Chad Smith and John Frusciante

Intro
Moderately ♩ = 102

Gtr. 1 (elec.)

*A   E   F♯m   A   E   F♯m

mf
w/ clean tone & phaser

*Chord symbols reflect basic harmony.

Verse

2nd & 3rd times, Gtr. 2 tacet

A   E   F♯m   A   E   F♯m

1. My name is Ve-ron-i-ca.   I come from the South Side of Chi-ca-go.
2. My name is Ne-bras-ka.   I live in a match-box of O-ma-ha.
3. My name is "I love you."   I come from the same place as ev-'ry-one.

Gtr. 1   **Riff A**

A   E   F♯m   B   D

Re-mem-ber my rain-coat.
It's noth-ing fan-tas-tic.   We love you the same way, yeah.
Just luck-y to be here.

End Riff A   **Rhy. Fig. 1**   **End Rhy. Fig. 1**

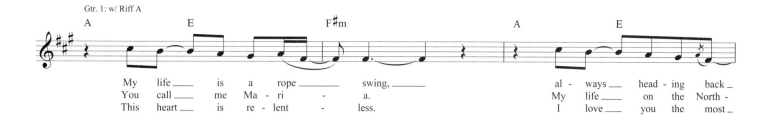

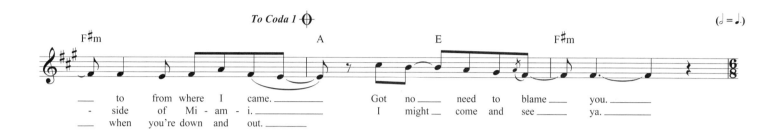

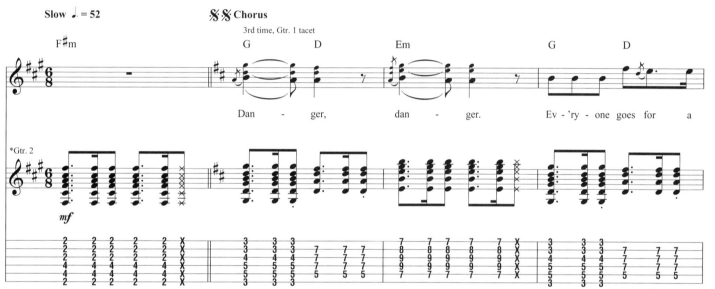

*3 gtrs. arr. for one (1 gtr. (elec.) w/ clean tone & 2 acous. gtrs.)

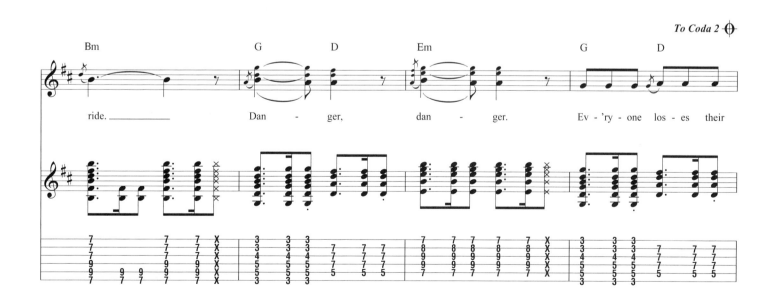

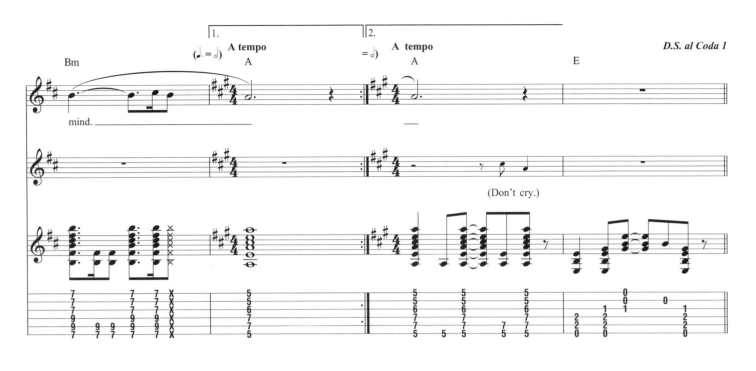

D.S. al Coda 1

(Don't cry.)

Coda 1

D.S.S. al Coda 2

Please come to my sens - es _____ 'cause we all ___ play the same game.

Coda 2

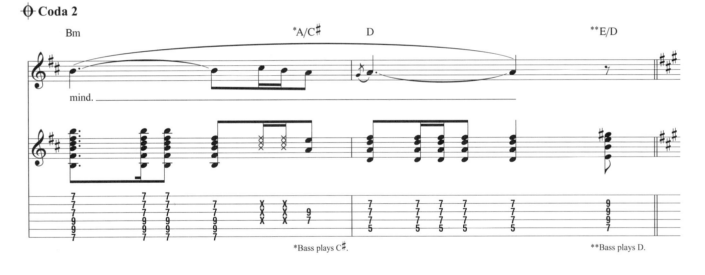

mind.

*Bass plays C#.   **Bass plays D.

Outro

Gtr. 2 tacet

Been a long time now. ___ Been a long time now. ___ Been a long time since I took you my toll.

Riff B

***Gtr. 3 (elec.)

w/ slight dist.

let ring ------   let ring ------   let ring ------

***Doubled throughout

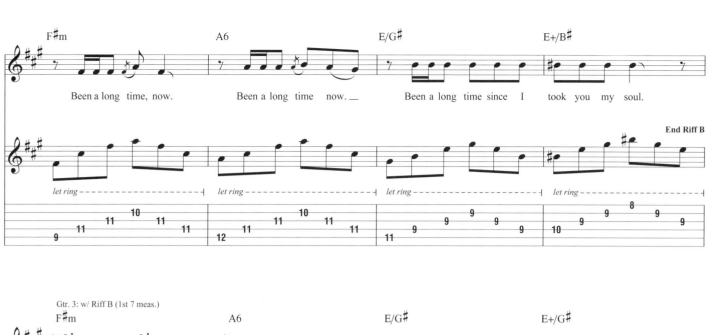

Been a long time, now. Been a long time now. Been a long time since I took you my soul.

End Riff B

Gtr. 3: w/ Riff B (1st 7 meas.)

I don't want it to be bro-ken up.

I don't want it to be with-out love.

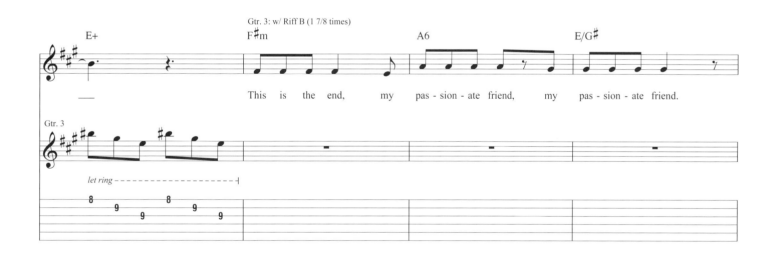

Gtr. 3: w/ Riff B (1 7/8 times)

This is the end, my pas-sion-ate friend, my pas-sion-ate friend.

Gtr. 3

Pass-ing on love for now. This is the end, my pas-sion-ate friend, my pas-sion-ate friend.

Gtr. 4 (elec.)

w/ dist.

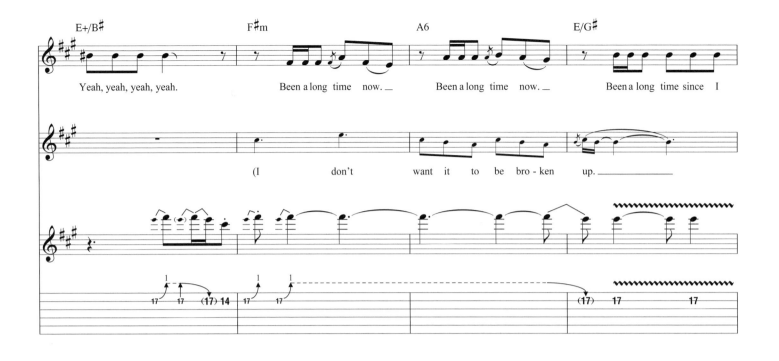

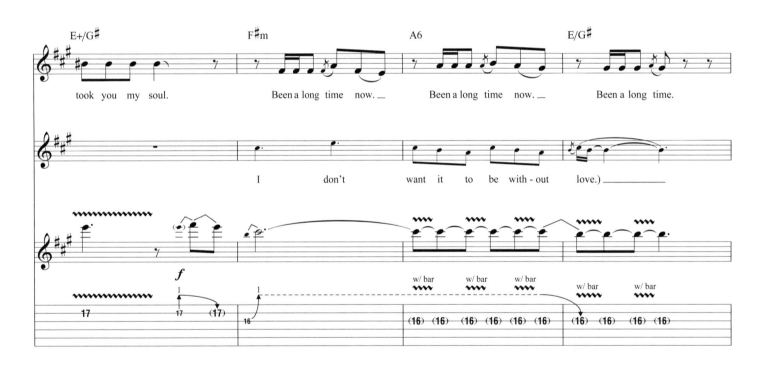

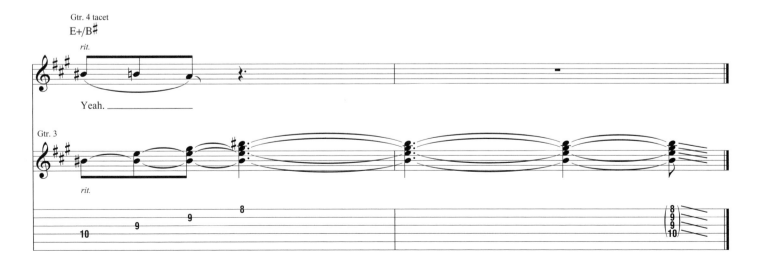

Let 'Em Cry

Words and Music by Anthony Kiedis, Flea, Chad Smith and John Frusciante

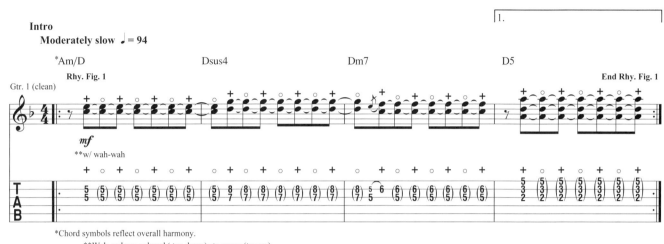

Intro
Moderately slow ♩ = 94

*Chord symbols reflect overall harmony.
**Wah-wah: ○ = closed (toe down); + = open (toe up)

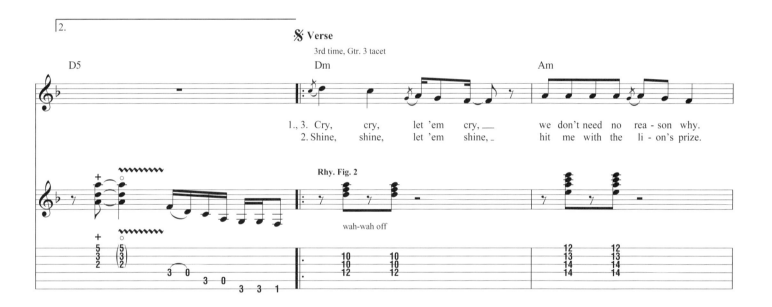

1., 3. Cry, cry, let 'em cry,___ we don't need no rea-son why.
2. Shine, shine, let 'em shine,___ hit me with the li-on's prize.

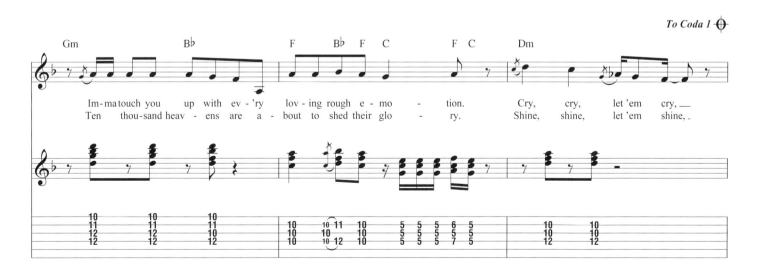

Im-ma touch you up with ev-'ry lov-ing rough e-mo- tion. Cry, cry, let 'em cry,___
Ten thou-sand heav-ens are a-bout to shed their glo- ry. Shine, shine, let 'em shine,___

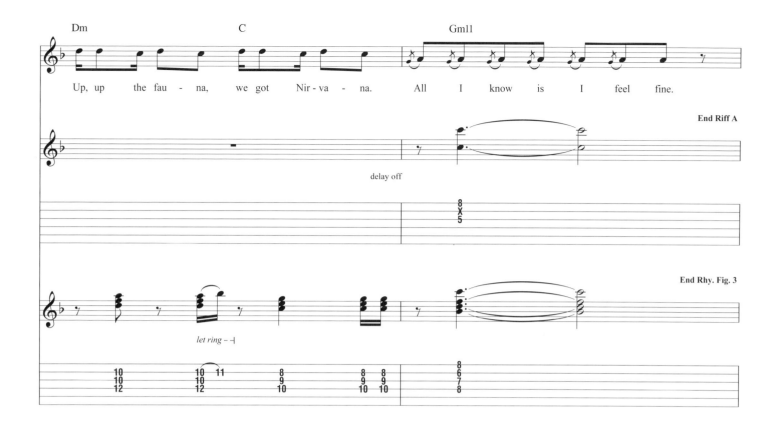

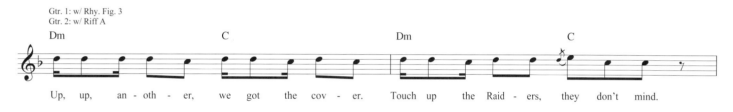

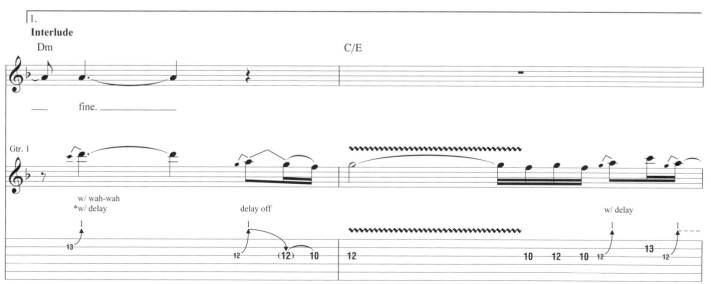

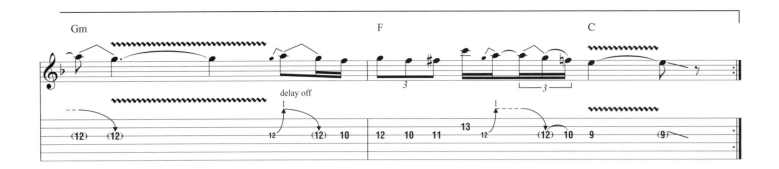

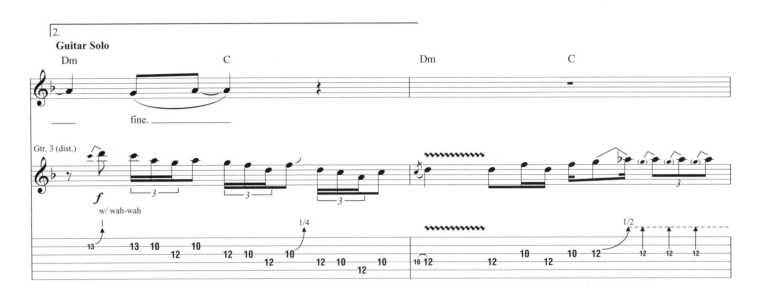

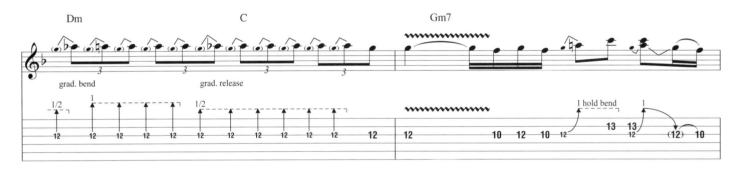

D.S. al Coda 1

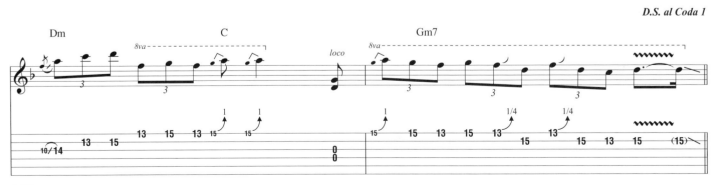

⊕ Coda 1

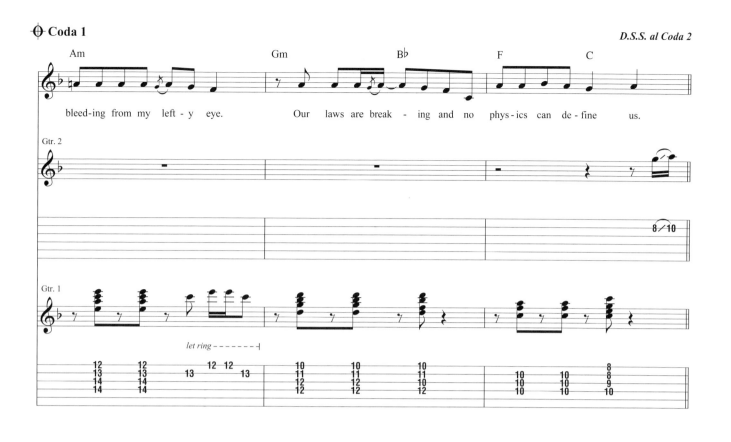

bleed-ing from my left - y eye.   Our laws are break - ing and no phys-ics can de-fine   us.

⊕ Coda 2

Interlude

Outro-Guitar Solo

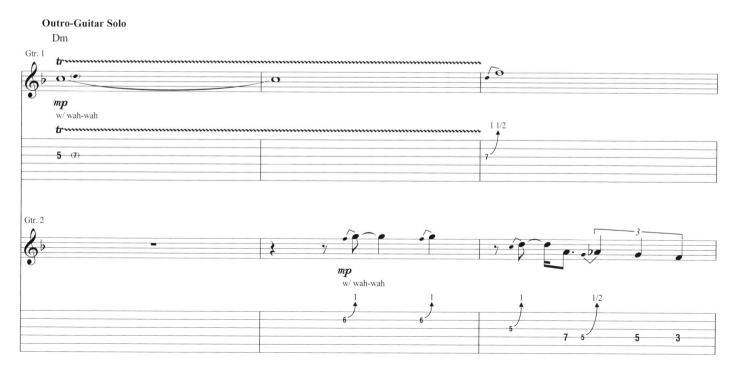

The Heavy Wing

Words and Music by Anthony Kiedis, Flea, Chad Smith and John Frusciante

Intro
Moderately ♩ = 101

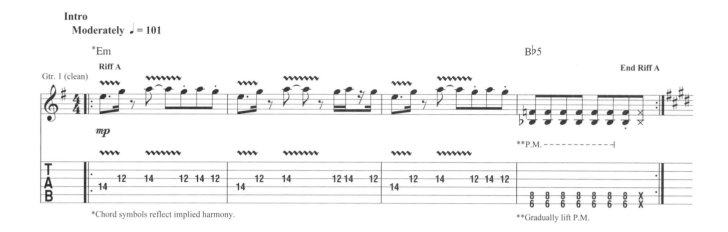

*Chord symbols reflect implied harmony.

**Gradually lift P.M.

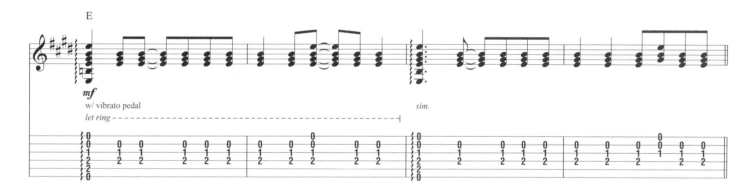

w/ vibrato pedal

let ring

sim.

Verse

2nd time, Gtr. 2 tacet

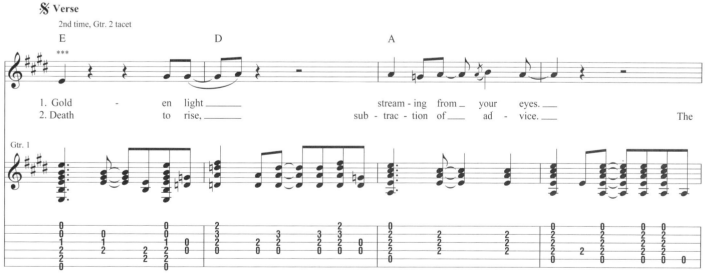

1. Gold — en light _____ stream - ing from _ your eyes. _____
2. Death to rise, _____ sub - trac - tion of ___ ad - vice. _____ The

Gtr. 1

***w/ echo set for quarter-note regeneration w/ 1 repeat.

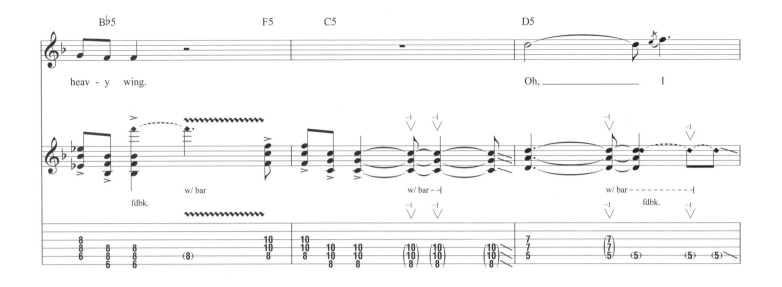

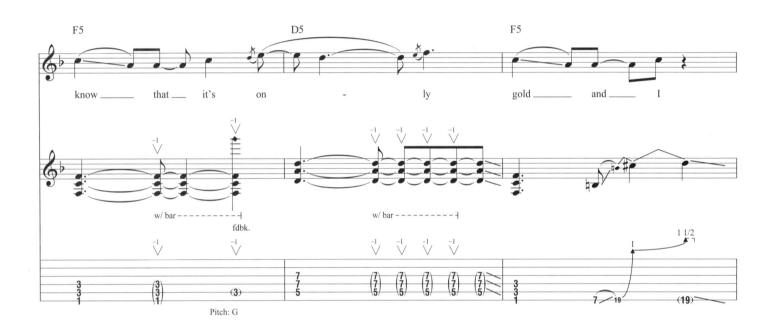

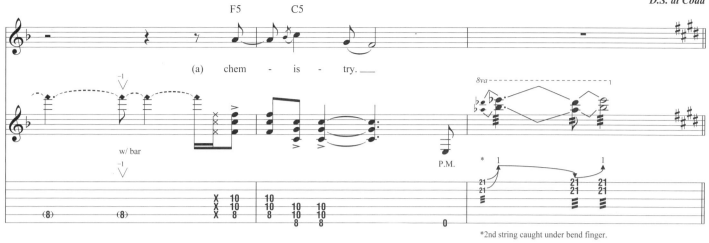

(a) chem - is - try. ____

*2nd string caught under bend finger.

⊕ **Coda**

Chorus

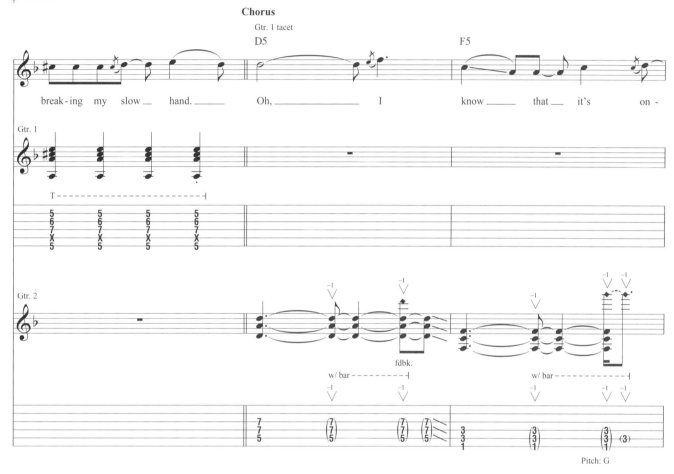

break-ing my slow ____ hand. ____ Oh, ____ I know ____ that ____ it's on -

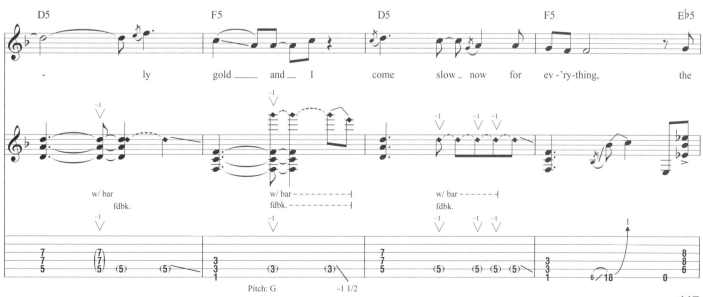

- ly gold ____ and ____ I come slow ____ now for ev -'ry-thing, the

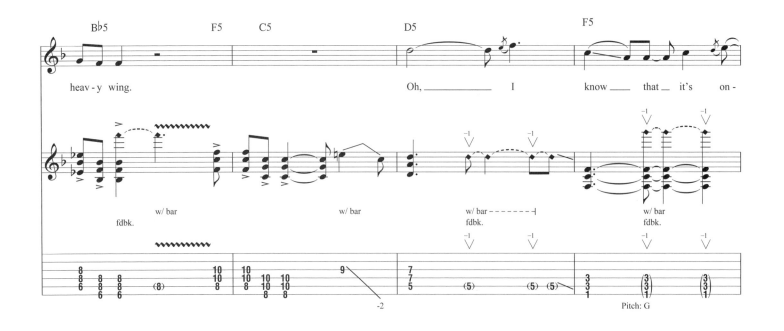

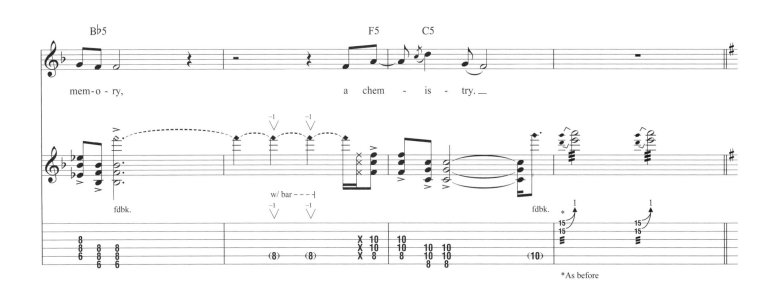

Interlude

*Gtr. 1: w/ Riff A

Guitar Solo

*w/ ring modulator   **Vol. swell   ***Chord symbols implied by bass.

*Refers to fdbk. only.

Tangelo

Words and Music by Anthony Kiedis, Flea, Chad Smith and John Frusciante

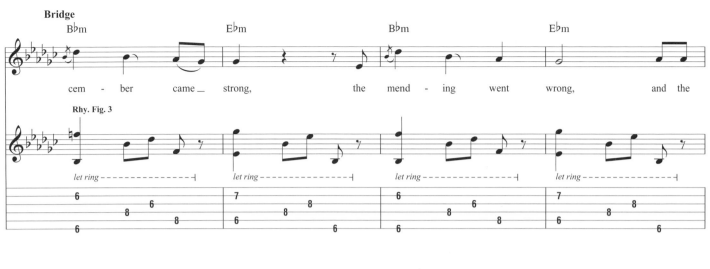

Bridge

cem - ber came __ strong, the mend - ing went wrong, and the

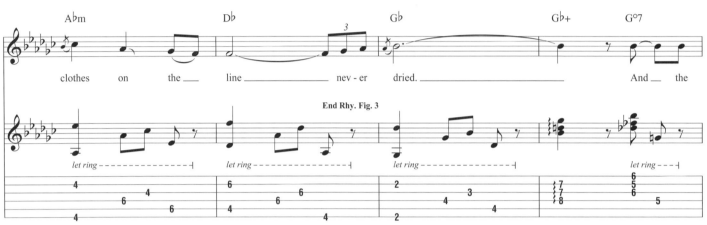

clothes on the __ line __ nev - er dried. __ And __ the

Gtr. 1: w/ Rhy. Fig. 3

crows on my __ hill came in for the __ kill, but the dream of this

D.S. al Coda

Interlude

Gtr. 1: w/ Rhy. Fig. 1

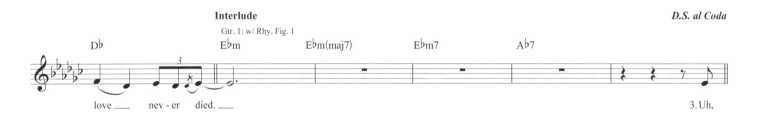

love __ nev - er died. __

3. Uh,

Coda

Outro

Let's pray.

GUITAR NOTATION LEGEND

Guitar music can be notated three different ways: on a *musical staff*, in *tablature*, and in *rhythm slashes*.

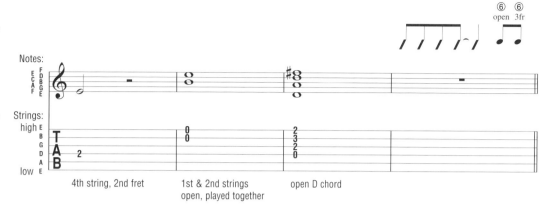

RHYTHM SLASHES are written above the staff. Strum chords in the rhythm indicated. Use the chord diagrams found at the top of the first page of the transcription for the appropriate chord voicings. Round noteheads indicate single notes.

THE MUSICAL STAFF shows pitches and rhythms and is divided by bar lines into measures. Pitches are named after the first seven letters of the alphabet.

TABLATURE graphically represents the guitar fingerboard. Each horizontal line represents a string, and each number represents a fret.

4th string, 2nd fret | 1st & 2nd strings open, played together | open D chord

Definitions for Special Guitar Notation

HALF-STEP BEND: Strike the note and bend up 1/2 step.

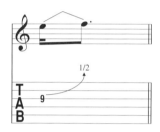

WHOLE-STEP BEND: Strike the note and bend up one step.

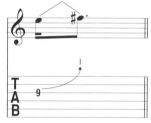

GRACE NOTE BEND: Strike the note and immediately bend up as indicated.

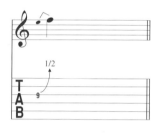

SLIGHT (MICROTONE) BEND: Strike the note and bend up 1/4 step.

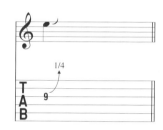

BEND AND RELEASE: Strike the note and bend up as indicated, then release back to the original note. Only the first note is struck.

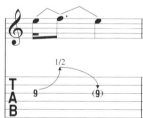

PRE-BEND: Bend the note as indicated, then strike it.

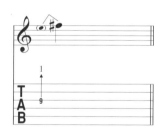

PRE-BEND AND RELEASE: Bend the note as indicated. Strike it and release the bend back to the original note.

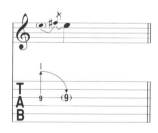

UNISON BEND: Strike the two notes simultaneously and bend the lower note up to the pitch of the higher.

VIBRATO: The string is vibrated by rapidly bending and releasing the note with the fretting hand.

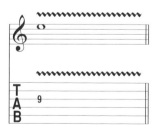

WIDE VIBRATO: The pitch is varied to a greater degree by vibrating with the fretting hand.

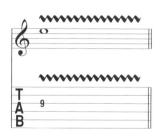

HAMMER-ON: Strike the first (lower) note with one finger, then sound the higher note (on the same string) with another finger by fretting it without picking.

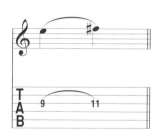

PULL-OFF: Place both fingers on the notes to be sounded. Strike the first note and without picking, pull the finger off to sound the second (lower) note.

LEGATO SLIDE: Strike the first note and then slide the same fret-hand finger up or down to the second note. The second note is not struck.

SHIFT SLIDE: Same as legato slide, except the second note is struck.

TRILL: Very rapidly alternate between the notes indicated by continuously hammering on and pulling off.

TAPPING: Hammer ("tap") the fret indicated with the pick-hand index or middle finger and pull off to the note fretted by the fret hand.

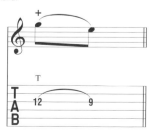

NATURAL HARMONIC: Strike the note while the fret-hand lightly touches the string directly over the fret indicated.

PINCH HARMONIC: The note is fretted normally and a harmonic is produced by adding the edge of the thumb or the tip of the index finger of the pick hand to the normal pick attack.

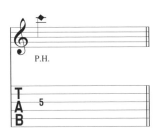

HARP HARMONIC: The note is fretted normally and a harmonic is produced by gently resting the pick hand's index finger directly above the indicated fret (in parentheses) while the pick hand's thumb or pick assists by plucking the appropriate string.

PICK SCRAPE: The edge of the pick is rubbed down (or up) the string, producing a scratchy sound.

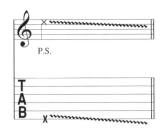

MUFFLED STRINGS: A percussive sound is produced by laying the fret hand across the string(s) without depressing, and striking them with the pick hand.

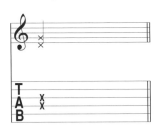

PALM MUTING: The note is partially muted by the pick hand lightly touching the string(s) just before the bridge.

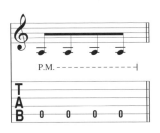

RAKE: Drag the pick across the strings indicated with a single motion.

TREMOLO PICKING: The note is picked as rapidly and continuously as possible.

ARPEGGIATE: Play the notes of the chord indicated by quickly rolling them from bottom to top.

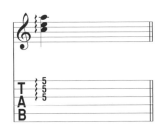

VIBRATO BAR DIVE AND RETURN: The pitch of the note or chord is dropped a specified number of steps (in rhythm), then returned to the original pitch.

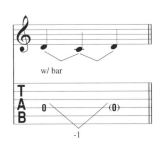

VIBRATO BAR SCOOP: Depress the bar just before striking the note, then quickly release the bar.

VIBRATO BAR DIP: Strike the note and then immediately drop a specified number of steps, then release back to the original pitch.

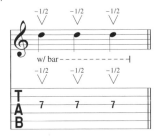

Additional Musical Definitions

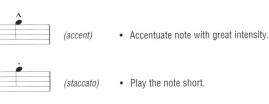 (accent)	•	Accentuate note (play it louder).
(accent)	•	Accentuate note with great intensity.
(staccato)	•	Play the note short.
⊓	•	Downstroke
V	•	Upstroke
D.S. al Coda	•	Go back to the sign (%), then play until the measure marked "*To Coda*," then skip to the section labelled "**Coda**."
D.C. al Fine	•	Go back to the beginning of the song and play until the measure marked "*Fine*" (end).

Rhy. Fig.	• Label used to recall a recurring accompaniment pattern (usually chordal).
Riff	• Label used to recall composed, melodic lines (usually single notes) which recur.
Fill	• Label used to identify a brief melodic figure which is to be inserted into the arrangement.
Rhy. Fill	• A chordal version of a Fill.
tacet	• Instrument is silent (drops out).
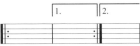	• Repeat measures between signs.
	• When a repeated section has different endings, play the first ending only the first time and the second ending only the second time.

NOTE: Tablature numbers in parentheses mean:
1. The note is being sustained over a system (note in standard notation is tied), or
2. The note is sustained, but a new articulation (such as a hammer-on, pull-off, slide or vibrato) begins, or
3. The note is a barely audible "ghost" note (note in standard notation is also in parentheses).

GUITAR RECORDED VERSIONS®

AUTHENTIC TRANSCRIPTIONS WITH NOTES AND TABLATURE

Guitar Recorded Versions® are note-for-note transcriptions of guitar music taken directly off recordings. This series, one of the most popular in print today, features some of the greatest guitar players and groups from blues and rock to country and jazz.

Guitar Recorded Versions are transcribed by the best transcribers in the business. Every book contains notes and tablature unless otherwise marked. Visit **halleonard.com** for our complete selection.

Will Ackerman
00690016 The Will Ackerman Collection $24.99
Bryan Adams
00690501 Greatest Hits $24.99
Aerosmith
00690603 O Yeah! $29.99
Alice in Chains
00690178 Acoustic $22.99
00694865 Dirt $19.99
00660225 Facelift $19.99
00694925 Jar of Flies/Sap $19.99
00690387 Nothing Safe $24.99
All That Remains
00142819 The Order of Things $22.99
Allman Brothers Band
00694932 Definitive Collection, Volume 1 $29.99
00694933 Definitive Collection, Volume 2 $27.99
00694934 Definitive Collection, Volume 3 $29.99
Duane Allman
00690958 Guitar Anthology $29.99
Alter Bridge
00691071 AB III $29.99
00690945 Blackbird $24.99
00690755 One Day Remains $24.99
Anthrax
00690849 Best of Anthrax $27.99
Arctic Monkeys
00123558 AM $24.99
Chet Atkins
00690158 Almost Alone $22.99
00694878 Vintage Fingerstyle $19.99
Audioslave
00690609 Audioslave $24.99
00690884 Revelations $19.95
Avenged Sevenfold
00690926 Avenged Sevenfold $24.99
00214869 Best of: 2005-2013 $29.99
00690820 City of Evil $27.99
00123216 Hail to the King $22.99
00691051 Nightmare $27.99
00222486 The Stage $29.99
00691065 Waking the Fallen $24.99
The Avett Brothers
00123140 Guitar Collection $22.99
Randy Bachman
00694918 Guitar Collection $24.99
The Beatles
00690489 1 (Number Ones) $24.99
00694929 1962-1966 $27.99
00694930 1967-1970 $29.99
00694880 Abbey Road $19.99
00694832 Acoustic Guitar $27.99
00691066 Beatles for Sale $22.99
00690903 Capitol Albums Vol. 2 $24.99
00691031 Help! $19.99
00690482 Let It Be $19.99
00691030 Magical Mystery Tour $22.99
00691067 Meet the Beatles! $22.99
00691068 Please Please Me $22.99
00694891 Revolver $22.99
00691014 Rock Band $34.99
00694914 Rubber Soul $24.99
00694863 Sgt. Pepper's Lonely Hearts Club Band $22.99
00110193 Tomorrow Never Knows $22.99
00690110 White Album Book 1 $19.99
00690111 White Album Book 2 $19.99

The Beach Boys
00690503 Very Best $24.99
Beck
00690632 Beck – Sea Change $19.95
Jeff Beck
00691044 Best of Beck $24.99
00691042 Blow by Blow $22.99
00691041 Truth $19.99
00691043 Wired $19.99
George Benson
00694884 Best of $22.99
Chuck Berry
00692385 Chuck Berry $24.99
Billy Talent
00690835 Billy Talent $22.99
00690879 Billy Talent II $22.99
Black Crowes
00147787 Best of $24.99
The Black Keys
00129737 Turn Blue $22.99
Black Sabbath
00690149 Black Sabbath $19.99
00690901 Best of $22.99
00691010 Heaven and Hell $24.99
00690148 Master of Reality $19.99
00690142 Paranoid $17.99
00691045 Vol. 4 $22.99
00692200 We Sold Our Soul for Rock 'n' Roll $24.99
blink-182
00690389 Enema of the State $22.99
00690831 Greatest Hits $24.99
00691179 Neighborhoods $22.99
Michael Bloomfield
00148544 Guitar Anthology $24.99
Blue Öyster Cult
00690028 Cult Classics $22.99
Bon Jovi
00691074 Greatest Hits $24.99
Joe Bonamassa
00158600 Blues of Desperation $24.99
00139086 Different Shades of Blue $22.99
00198117 Muddy Wolf at Red Rocks $24.99
00283540 Redemption $24.99
00358863 Royal Tea $24.99
Boston
00690913 Boston $22.99
00690829 Guitar Collection $24.99
David Bowie
00690491 Best of $22.99
Box Car Racer
00690583 Box Car Racer $19.95
Breaking Benjamin
00691023 Dear Agony $22.99
00690873 Phobia $22.99
Lenny Breau
00141446 Best of $19.99
Big Bill Broonzy
00286503 Guitar Collection $19.99
Roy Buchanan
00690168 Collection $24.99
Jeff Buckley
00690451 Collection $27.99
Bullet for My Valentine
00690957 Scream Aim Fire $22.99
00119629 Temper Temper $22.99
Kenny Burrell
00690678 Best of $24.99
Cage the Elephant
00691077 Thank You, Happy Birthday $22.99

The Cars
00691159 Complete Greatest Hits $24.99
Carter Family
00690261 Collection $19.99
Johnny Cash
00691079 Best of $24.99
Cheap Trick
00690043 Best of $24.99
Chicago
00690171 Definitive Guitar Collection $29.99
Chimaira
00691011 Guitar Collection $24.99
Charlie Christian
00690567 Definitive Collection $22.99
Eric Church
00101916 Chief $22.99
The Civil Wars
00129545 The Civil Wars $19.99
Eric Clapton
00690590 Anthology $34.99
00694896 Blues Breakers (with John Mayall) $19.99
00138731 The Breeze $24.99
00691055 Clapton $22.99
00690936 Complete Clapton $34.99
00690010 From the Cradle $24.99
00192383 I Still Do $19.99
00690363 Just One Night $27.99
00694873 Timepieces $19.95
00694869 Unplugged $24.99
00124873 Unplugged (Deluxe) $29.99
The Clash
00690162 Best of $22.99
Coheed & Cambria
00690828 IV $24.99
00139967 In Keeping Secrets of Silent Earth: 3 $24.99
Coldplay
00130786 Ghost Stories $19.99
Collective Soul
00690855 Best of $19.95
Jessee Cook
00141704 Works Vol. 1 $19.99
Alice Cooper
00691091 Best of $24.99
Counting Crows
00694940 August & Everything After $22.99
Robert Cray
00127184 Best of $19.99
Cream
00694840 Disraeli Gears $24.99
Creed
00288787 Greatest Hits $22.99
Creedence Clearwater Revival
00690819 Best of $27.99
Jim Croce
00690648 The Very Best $19.99
Steve Cropper
00690572 Soul Man $22.99
Crosby, Stills & Nash
00690613 Best of $29.99
Cry of Love
00691171 Brother $22.99
Dick Dale
00690637 Best of $22.99
Death Cab for Cutie
00690967 Narrow Stairs $22.99
Deep Purple
00690289 Best of $22.99
00690288 Machine Head $19.99

Def Leppard
00690784 Best of $24.99
Derek and the Dominos
00694831 Layla & Other Assorted Love Songs $24.99
Ani DiFranco
00690384 Best of $19.95
Dinosaur Jr.
00690979 Best of $22.99
The Doors
00690347 Anthology $22.95
00690348 Essential Collection $16.95
Dream Theater
00160579 The Astonishing $24.99
00122443 Dream Theater $29.99
00291164 Distance Over Time $24.99
Eagles
00278631 Their Greatest Hits 1971-1975 $22.99
00278632 Very Best of $39.99
Duane Eddy
00690250 Best of $24.99
Tommy Emmanuel
00147067 All I Want for Christmas $19.99
00690909 Best of $27.99
00172824 It's Never Too Late $22.99
00139220 Little by Little $24.99
Melissa Etheridge
00690555 Best of $19.95
Evanescence
00691186 Evanescence $22.99
Extreme
00690515 Pornograffitti $24.99
John Fahey
00150257 Guitar Anthology $24.99
Tal Farlow
00125661 Best of $19.99
Five Finger Death Punch
00691009 5 Finger Death Punch $24.99
00691181 American Capitalism $22.99
00128917 Wrong Side of Heaven & Righteous Side of Hell $22.99
Fleetwood Mac
00690664 Best of $24.99
Flyleaf
00690870 Flyleaf $19.95
Foghat
00690986 Best of $22.99
Foo Fighters
00691024 Greatest Hits $24.99
00691115 Wasting Light $24.99
Peter Frampton
00690842 Best of $22.99
Robben Ford
00690805 Best of $24.99
00120220 Guitar Anthology $29.99
Free
00694920 Best of $24.99
Rory Gallagher
00295410 Blues (Selections) $24.99
Danny Gatton
00694807 88 Elmira St $24.99
Genesis
00690438 Guitar Anthology $24.99
Godsmack
00120167 Godsmack $19.95
00691048 The Oracle $22.99
Goo Goo Dolls
00690943 Greatest Hits Vol. 1 $24.99
Grateful Dead
00139460 Guitar Anthology $34.99

Green Day
00212480 Revolution Radio $19.99
00118259 ¡Tré! $21.99
00113073 ¡Uno! $21.99
Peter Green
00691190 Best of $24.99
Greta Van Fleet
00287517 Anthem of the Peaceful Army $22.99
00287515 From the Fires $19.99
Patty Griffin
00690927 Children Running Through $19.95
Guns N' Roses
00690978 Chinese Democracy $24.99
Buddy Guy
00691027 Anthology $24.99
00694854 Damn Right, I've Got the Blues $19.95
Jim Hall
00690697 Best of $22.99
Ben Harper
00690840 Both Sides of the Gun $19.95
00691018 Fight for Your Mind $22.99
George Harrison
00694798 Anthology $24.99
Scott Henderson
00690841 Blues Guitar Collection $24.99
Jimi Hendrix
00692930 Are You Experienced? $29.99
00692931 Axis: Bold As Love $24.99
00690304 Band of Gypsys $27.99
00690608 Blue Wild Angel $24.95
00275044 Both Sides of the Sky $22.99
00692932 Electric Ladyland $27.99
00690017 Live at Woodstock $29.99
00119619 People, Hell & Angels $27.99
00690602 Smash Hits $24.99
00691152 West Coast Seattle Boy (Anthology) $29.99
00691332 Winterland $22.99
H.I.M.
00690843 Dark Light $19.95
Buddy Holly
00660029 Best of $24.99
John Lee Hooker
00690793 Anthology $29.99
Howlin' Wolf
00694905 Howlin' Wolf $22.99
Billy Idol
00690692 Very Best of $24.99
Imagine Dragons
00121961 Night Visions $22.99
Incubus
00690688 A Crow Left of the Murder $19.95
Iron Maiden
00690790 Anthology $27.99
00691058 The Final Frontier $22.99
00200446 Guitar Tab $34.99
Alan Jackson
00690730 Guitar Collection $29.99
Elmore James
00694938 Master of the Electric Slide Guitar $19.99
Jane's Addiction
00690652 Best of $24.99
Jethro Tull
00690684 Aqualung $24.99
00690693 Guitar Anthology $24.99
00691182 Stand Up $22.99

John 5
00690898 The Devil Knows
My Name..................$22.95
00690814 Songs for Sanity.........$19.95
00690751 Vertigo $19.95
Eric Johnson
00694912 Ah Via Musicom $24.99
00690660 Best of......................$29.99
00691076 Up Close...................$22.99
00690169 Venus Isle...................$29.99
Robert Johnson
00690271 New Transcriptions ...$27.99
Janis Joplin
00699131 Best of......................$24.99
Judas Priest
00690427 Best of......................$24.99
Kansas
00690277 Best of......................$24.99
Phil Keaggy
00690911 Best of......................$24.99
Toby Keith
00690727 Guitar Collection $19.99
The Killers
00690910 Sam's Town $19.95
Killswitch Engage
00120814 Disarm the Descent...$22.99
Albert King
00690504 Very Best of...............$24.99
00124869 In Session $24.99
B.B. King
00690430 Anthology...................$29.99
00130447 Live at the Regal........$19.99
00690444 Riding with the King ..$24.99
Freddie King
00690134 Collection..................$22.99
Marcus King
00327968 El Dorado $22.99
Kiss
00690157 Alive! $19.99
00690356 Alive II $24.99
00694903 Best of......................$29.99
00690355 Destroyer $19.99
00291163 Very Best of $24.99
Mark Knopfler
00690164 Guitar Styles $27.99
Greg Koch
00345767 Best of......................$29.99
Korn
00690780 Greatest Hits Vol. 1....$24.99
Kris Kristofferson
00690377 Collection..................$22.99
Lamb of God
00690834 Ashes of the Wake $24.99
00691187 Resolution $22.99
00690875 Sacrament $24.99
Ray LaMontagne
00690977 Gossip in the Grain ...$19.99
00691057 God Willin' & The
Creek Don't Rise $22.99
John Lennon
00690679 Guitar Collection $27.99
Linkin Park
00690922 Minutes to Midnight ..$22.99
The Lumineers
00114563 The Lumineers $22.99
George Lynch
00690525 Best of......................$29.99
Lynyrd Skynyrd
00690955 All-Time Greatest Hits. $24.99
00694954 New Best of $24.99
Yngwie Malmsteen
00690577 Anthology...................$29.99
Marilyn Manson
00690754 Lest We Forget...........$22.99
Bob Marley
00694956 Legend $22.99
00694945 Songs of Freedom $29.99
Pat Martino
00139168 Guitar Anthology $29.99
John McLaughlin
00129105 Guitar Tab Anthology...$27.99
Mastodon
00690989 Crack the Skye $24.99
00236690 Emperor of Sand.......$22.99

00691176 The Hunter................$24.99
00137718 Once More 'Round
the Sun..............$24.99
Andy McKee
00691942 Art of Motion $24.99
00691034 Joyland $19.99
Don McLean
00120080 Songbook..................$22.99
Megadeth
00694952 Countdown to
Extinction.........$24.99
00691015 Endgame $27.99
00276065 Greatest Hits.............$27.99
00694951 Rust in Peace $27.99
00690011 Youthanasia $24.99
John Mellencamp
00690505 Guitar Collection $24.99
Metallica
00209876 Hardwired...
To Self-Destruct.........$24.99
Pat Metheny
00690562 Bright Size Life $24.99
00691073 Day Trip/
Tokyo Day Trip Live...$22.99
00690646 One Quiet Night.........$24.99
00690559 Question & Answer....$24.99
00690558 Trio 99-00 ....$24.99
00690561 Trio Live $27.99
00118836 Unity Band $22.99
00102590 What's It All About....$24.99
Steve Miller Band
00690040 Young Hearts: Complete
Greatest Hits.............$24.99
Ministry
00119338 Guitar Tab Collection ..$24.99
Wes Montgomery
00102591 Guitar Anthology $27.99
Gary Moore
00691092 Best of......................$27.99
00694802 Still Got the Blues......$24.99
Alanis Morissette
00355456 Jagged Little Pill $22.99
Motion City Soundtrack
00691005 Best of $19.99
Mountain
00694958 Best of $22.99
Mumford & Sons
00691070 Sigh No More $22.99
Muse
00118196 The 2nd Law $19.99
00151195 Drones......................$19.99
My Morning Jacket
00690996 Collection $19.99
Matt Nathanson
00690984 Some Mad Hope $22.99
Night Ranger
00690883 Best of $19.99
Nirvana
00690611 Nirvana....................$24.99
00694895 Bleach $19.99
00694913 In Utero $22.99
00694883 Nevermind...............$19.99
00690026 Unplugged
in New York $19.99
Nothing More
00265439 Guitar & Bass Tab
Collection..........$24.99
The Offspring
00690807 Greatest Hits.............$24.99
Opeth
00243349 Best of $22.99
Roy Orbison
00691052 Black & White Night..$22.99
Ozzy Osbourne
00694847 Best of......................$27.99
Brad Paisley
00690933 Best of......................$27.99
00690995 Play..........................$29.99
Christopher Parkening
00690939 Solo Pieces $24.99
Les Paul
00690594 Best of......................$24.99
Pearl Jam
00694855 Ten...........................$24.99

Periphery
00146043 Guitar Tab Collection..$24.99
Carl Perkins
00690725 Best of $19.99
Tom Petty
00690499 Definitive Collection ..$24.99
Phish
00690176 Billy Breathes $24.99
Pink Floyd
00121933 Acoustic Collection....$27.99
00690428 Dark Side of
the Moon $22.99
00142677 The Endless River......$19.99
00244637 Guitar Anthology $24.99
00239799 The Wall...................$27.99
Poison
00690789 Best of......................$22.99
Elvis Presley
00690299 King of Rock 'n' Roll.$22.99
Prince
00690925 Very Best of..............$24.99
Queen
00690003 Classic Queen............$24.99
00694975 Greatest Hits.............$25.99
Queens of the Stone Age
00254332 Villains $22.99
Queensryche
00690670 Very Best of..............$24.99
The Raconteurs
00690878 Broken Boy Soldiers...$19.95
Radiohead
00109303 Guitar Anthology $29.99
Rage Against the Machine
00694910 Rage Against the
Machine $24.99
00119834 Guitar Anthology $24.99
Rancid
00690179 And Out Come the
Wolves.....................$24.99
Ratt
00690426 Best of......................$24.99
Red Hot Chili Peppers
00690055 BloodSugarSexMagik..$19.99
00690584 By the Way $24.99
00690379 Californication...........$22.99
00182634 The Getaway.............$24.99
00690673 Greatest Hits.............$24.99
00691166 I'm with You..............$22.99
00690255 Mother's Milk............$19.95
00690090 One Hot Minute........$22.95
00690852 Stadium Arcadium.....$29.99
00706518 Unlimited Loved $27.99
Jerry Reed
00694892 Guitar Style of...........$24.99
Django Reinhardt
00690511 Definitive Collection ..$24.99
Jimmie Rodgers
00690260 Guitar Collection $22.99
Rolling Stones
00690014 Exile on Main Street..$24.99
00690631 Guitar Anthology $34.99
00694976 Some Girls $22.95
00690264 Tattoo You................$19.95
Angelo Romero
00690974 Bella.........................$19.99
David Lee Roth
00690685 Eat 'Em and Smile.....$24.99
00690942 Songs of Van Halen ...$19.95
Rush
00323854 The Spirit of Radio $22.99
Santana
00173534 Guitar Anthology $29.99
00690031 Greatest Hits.............$24.99
Joe Satriani
00276350 What Happens Next ..$24.99
Michael Schenker
00690796 Very Best of..............$24.99
Matt Schofield
00128870 Guitar Tab Collection ..$22.99
Scorpions
00690566 Best of......................$24.99
Bob Seger
00690604 Guitar Collection $24.99

Ed Sheeran
00234543 Divide......................$19.99
00138870 X..............................$19.99
Kenny Wayne Shepherd
00690803 Best of......................$24.99
00151178 Ledbetter Heights $19.99
Shinedown
00692433 Amaryllis $22.99
Skillet
00122218 Rise..........................$22.99
Slash
00691114 Guitar Anthology $34.99
Slayer
00690872 Christ Illusion $19.95
00690813 Guitar Collection $24.99
Slipknot
00690419 Slipknot....................$22.99
00690973 All Hope Is Gone $24.99
Smashing Pumpkins
00316982 Greatest Hits.............$24.99
Social Distortion
00690330 Live at the Roxy.........$24.99
Soundgarden
00690912 Guitar Anthology $24.99
Steely Dan
00120004 Best of......................$27.99
Steppenwolf
00694921 Best of......................$22.95
Mike Stern
00690655 Best of......................$27.99
Cat Stevens
14041588 Tea for the Tillerman..$19.99
Rod Stewart
00690949 Guitar Anthology $19.99
Stone Temple Pilots
00322564 Thank You.................$22.99
Styx
00690520 Guitar Collection $22.99
Sublime
00120081 Sublime....................$22.99
00120122 40 oz. to Freedom......$24.99
00690992 Robbin' the Hood.......$19.99
SUM 41
00690519 All Killer No Filler $19.95
00690929 Underclass Hero $19.95
Supertramp
00691072 Best of $24.99
Taylor Swift
00690994 Taylor Swift $22.99
00690993 Fearless....................$22.99
00115957 Red $21.99
00691063 Speak Now $22.99
System of a Down
00690531 Toxicity.....................$19.99
James Taylor
00694824 Best of $19.99
Thin Lizzy
00694887 Best of $22.99
.38 Special
00690988 Guitar Anthology $22.99
Three Days Grace
00691039 Life Starts Now $22.99
Trans-Siberian Orchestra
00150209 Guitar Anthology $19.99
Merle Travis
00690233 Collection.................$24.99
Trivium
00253237 Guitar Tab Anthology...$24.99
00123862 Vengeance Falls $24.99
Robin Trower
00690683 Bridge of Sighs..........$19.99
U2
00699191 Best of: 1980-1990 ..$24.99
00690732 Best of: 1990-2000 ...$29.99
00690894 18 Singles $24.99

Keith Urban
00124461 Guitar Anthology $29.99
Steve Vai
00690039 Alien Love Secrets $24.99
00690575 Alive in an
Ultra World..............$22.95
00690172 Fire Garden..............$34.99
00156024 Guitar Anthology $39.99
00197570 Modern Primitive $29.99
00660137 Passion & Warfare......$29.99
00690881 Real Illusions:
Reflections...........$27.99
00690605 The Elusive Light
and Sound, Vol. 1......$29.99
00694904 Sex and Religion $24.95
00110385 The Story of Light......$24.99
00690392 The Ultra Zone $19.95
Van Halen
00700555 Van Halen $22.99
00295076 30 Classics $29.99
00700092 1984 ....$24.99
00700558 Fair Warning $24.99
Stevie Ray Vaughan
00690024 Couldn't Stand
the Weather............$22.99
00690116 Guitar Collection $29.99
00694879 In the Beginning........$19.95
00660136 In Step $24.99
00660058 Lightnin' Blues 83-87. $29.99
00690550 Live at Montreux $29.99
00217455 Plays Slow Blues........$24.99
00694835 The Sky Is Crying $24.99
00690025 Soul to Soul.............$19.95
00690015 Texas Flood..............$22.99
Volbeat
00109770 Guitar Collection $24.99
00121808 Outlaw Gentlemen
& Shady Ladies......$24.99
T-Bone Walker
00690132 Collection..................$22.99
Muddy Waters
00694789 Deep Blues $27.99
Doc Watson
00152161 Guitar Anthology $24.99
Weezer
00690071 The Blue Album $22.99
00691046 Rarities Edition $22.99
Paul Westerberg & The Replacements
00691036 Very Best of..............$19.99
The White Stripes
00237811 Greatest Hits.............$24.99
Whitesnake
00117511 Guitar Collection $24.99
The Who
00691941 Acoustic Guitar
Collection..........$22.99
00690447 Best of $24.99
Wilco
00691006 Guitar Collection $24.99
The Yardbirds
00690596 Best of......................$22.99
Yes
00122303 Guitar Collection $24.99
Dwight Yoakam
00690916 Best of $22.99
Frank Zappa
00690507 Apostrophe................$22.99
00690443 Hot Rats $22.99
00690624 One Size Fits All $27.99
00690623 Over-Nite Sensation ..$24.99
ZZ Top
00121684 Early Classics $27.99
00690589 Guitar Anthology $24.99
00690960 Guitar Classics $24.99